# HOW TO MEET AND HANG OUT WITH THE

# STARS

 *A Totally Unauthorized Guide*

# HOW TO MEET AND HANG OUT WITH THE STARS

## Bret Saxon and Steve Stein

A CITADEL PRESS BOOK

*Published by Carol Publishing Group*

A Citadel Press Book
Published by Carol Publishing Group
Citadel Press is a registered trademark of Carol Communications,
  Inc.
Editorial Offices: 600 Madison Avenue, New York, N.Y. 10022
Sales and Distribution Offices: 120 Enterprise Avenue, Secaucus,
  N.J. 07094
In Canada: Canadian Manda Group, One Atlantic Avenue, Suite 105,
  Toronto, Ontario M6K 3E7
Queries regarding rights and permissions should be addressed to
Carol Publishing Group, 600 Madison Avenue, New York, N.Y. 10022

Carol Publishing Books are available at special discounts for
bulk purchases, sales promotion, fund-raising, or educational
purposes. Special editions can be created to specifications. For
details, contact: Special Sales Department, Carol Publishing
Group, 120 Enterprise Avenue, Secaucus, NJ 07094.

MANUFACTURED IN THE UNITED STATES OF AMERICA

10  9  8  7  6  5  4  3  2  1

Library of Congress Cataloging-in-Publication Data
Saxon, Bret.
    How to meet and hang out with the stars : a totally unauthorized
guide / Bret Saxon and Steve Stein.
       p.   cm.
    "A Citadel Press book."
    ISBN 0-8065-1683-6 (pbk.)
    1. Motion picture actors and actresses—Home and haunts—United
States.   2. Celebrities—Homes and haunts—United States.
1. Stein, Steve, 1965–    . II. Title.
PN1993.5.U6S314   1995
791.43′028′092273—dc20                                    95-19252
                                                             CIP

# Contents

# Acknowledgments

## *Thanks Everyone*

We would like to give **Golden Wackerman Awards** to the following people, places, and things, without whose help and support over the years, we would have done this book anyway: Bill "our first camera" Giavelli, "The Devious" Clara Hall, Lynda, Rae, Myron, Lenny "quick legitimate score" S., Larry D., Carol from Subway, Scott "no meat" S., Dr. Walk and his "lovely" family, Mr. Sleep and catalog his records and his family, Carolyn and Roger, Tracy, Pappy and Judith Carol, Zzyzx, Schwartzy "did you guys have pizza on the way over here?" Schwartzman, the Chonus mobiles ('67 six slanty), chukiako, Don Knotts, Pacer and Gremlin (X), Two Guys from Italy pizza in Hollywood, "rack 'em off" Elkouby, Norena Barbella, Herbie, Floyd, Mickey, Boomer Seymore, Eugenie, Gigi, Hyman, Great Granny Franny, Granny from New York, Ida, Nana Ana, Max, brown sugar cinnamon Pop-Tarts, the Friday-night poker gang, blankie, baba-milk, Jana, Mark, Mary, Richard, Auntie Tea, Aunt "shepherd's pie" Shirley, Phill "two *L*'s" Swagel songs, "They're not saying boo, they're saying" Lou, Aunt Lil from New Jersey, Notes from Nova, Come on Baby, Flutter, Flutter, Flutter, Hong Kong Phooey, the carwash, Fred from Yermo, Nuncha, your face, The Nuclear Grand Saxongale system, Queen, Macias, Tripper, John Winger, SSSSadie and Sam, Knott's Berry Farm, Hard Rock Cafe, Planet Hollywood, Dic Dic, Kenny "all access and how many more do you need" S., Megan, David, Kerry, Greg, Dusty, Kip, Ron "I don't like to pick up on nuns" Finklestein, Bubba and Buford, Chelsey and JJ, the Kershbergs and Grandma's potato salad, Mr. CAA

Matthew Snyder, Rae's chopped liver, all in Big Bear, "You're pickin' from the bottom of da barrel", Bronchial Spasm and Johnathan, Arnold Ziffel, Regis and Kathie Lee, Theodore "Ted" $825, the TR7, Oakwood, Key Tag and Spanky, Barney Rubble, Chamadeesh, Amanat, Wally, Schmool, The Body Shop with magic by Shamada, Steven Glassman, Seymore Arfin and Matty, Larry H. Parker, Graham the Ticket Man, the Lady Lee closet, Foy, Leahhhh, Lenny Benson, the Dufec twins, Jill Covington, Kim Sorenson, Debbie Kurtela, Barbara Roper, everyone at Computax, Dr. Savache, Rod and all at Dadson, Parasol, ACMC, Southland FCU, D.A.C., Bubba, Jack, Don M. at AWA, BPSD, Sharon Le Nails, Radisson Empire, Leah, Steve, Tina, Lee Hoffman, Jackie Levin, Kathy Palmerino, Heidi Dahman, Mimi Pitzi, Laughlin bus trips, QRFEBSSSATB, Adolf—whose frisbee hit his woman, Lighten' up Francis, the loofah, Bobbi Brown, cranberry juice, L. Ron "sounds kind of awkward," Mad Dog, Phillbert, Thumbs Up Bruce, I've been Mertzed, Mikey G and family, Joe Seimper de Fi, Hackenback, George "producer of Arnold Schwarzenegger's *The Running Man*" Linder, Ann B. Davis, Mrs. Cydny Starpuck, Larry "Bud" Melman, the shrimp industry, superagent Hermann Lademann, a special thanks to Elvis, and most of all, Jill, Michele, Brittney, Brianne, and Ryan.

We'd also like to present **Golden Plop Awards** to those that had a different type of impact: Mrs. Kenny, Norma "I'll say no on Mr. Trump's behalf" Foerderer, Ringo Starr, Ed Levin, Magic Johnson, California Games, Orris, Jim Fagston, and Greg at PH.

# HOW TO MEET
# AND HANG OUT
# WITH THE

# 1

## Introduction

**H**ere is something to keep in mind: We're nobody. Steve and I have never had legitimate reasons for being in the places we've been and meeting the people we've met, yet we've met a ridiculous number of celebrities. Sometimes it's been by chance, other times by scheming and plotting and using all the tricks we know—usually through a combination of both. In the final analysis, we've had fun, we've met some pretty famous people, and we've got some interesting stories to tell.

My name is Bret Saxon. In this book, my partner Steve Stein and I will tell you some of these fantastic stories of our experiences meeting and hanging out with the famous and celebrated. More than that, we will show you how you can do this too. We will give you the tools you need to meet the celebrities—*any celebrities*. We will guide you through the steps to get yourself and your friends invited to all the big events and parties. You will learn how to find stars, how to mingle comfortably with them, what to say when you finally come face-to-face with your idols, and even how to make some money along the way.

Have you ever dreamed of what it would be like to sit in the audience at the Academy Awards, among the most famous people in the world, instead of just watching it on your television?

Have you ever fantasized about being at a fabulous Hollywood party where you run into Tom Cruise, Julia Roberts, Clint Eastwood, or Sharon Stone, and they invite you to sit down at their table?

Perhaps you've always wanted to walk backstage after a Billy Joel concert and rave to the Piano Man about what a great singer he is.

Or maybe you'd give anything just to stand on the sidelines at the Superbowl and listen to the talk between the players on the bench.

These no longer have to be dreams. All of these adventures, plus many more, can be reality if you just learn the secrets revealed in this book. Almost everyone has a hidden desire to be famous, to live in the world of celebrity—or at least be associated with it—but few get the opportunity. Wouldn't it be wonderful to join that world, to be invited to the world premieres, the awards shows, the backstage parties? The advice in this book will ensure that you will be among the chosen few to participate in the hottest celebrity events in the world.

Keep in mind that Steve and I are not affiliated with the entertainment industry in any way. However, over the course of the last eleven years we have enjoyed many of the top celebrity events around the country. How did we do it? How did we obtain the invitations? This book will take you through the process of obtaining invitations to a myriad of occasions.

Picture yourself discussing the political implications of the Rambo films with Sylvester Stallone at the groundbreaking of his new business, or pitching your latest business idea to Donald Trump at a fundraiser held at a posh New York restaurant (the food is complimentary). Whatever your dreams or interests, they can be realized if you follow the easy steps laid out in this book.

This book will teach you how to:

- Obtain free press kits of your favorite movies, which include biography information, 8x10 glossy photos, movie descriptions,and free giveaways
- Obtain free press kits for your favorite musical groups
- Secure a place on the guest lists of such events as:
    the Academy Awards
    the Grammy Awards
    the American Music Awards
    Celebrity fund-raisers
    Movie premieres
- Obtain backstage passes for concerts and special events
- Learn of industry trade shows and other important celebrity appearances

Bret and Steve enjoying a moment onstage behind the podium at the
Grammy Awards.

- Obtain perks such as free tuxedos and limousines
- Create business opportunities such as band management or artist
  promotion

This book will open important doors for you. You will be able to
talk to major celebrities you have admired for years. Read this book
carefully, follow the steps outlined, and have the time of your life.

# 2

## Brushes With Greatness

**A**s you begin to utilize the methods outlined in this book, you will find yourself face-to-face with the most famous people in the world. Whatever your interests, from teenage heartthrobs such as Joey Lawrence to business giants such as Disney CEO Michael Eisner, this book will tell you how to locate and meet your favorite personalities. Your stories of these meetings will entertain your family and impress your friends and coworkers. Picture yourself going to school and describing how you met Michael Jackson the night before. It's incredible. What follows in this chapter are a few of our stories.

### The 1992 Emmy Awards

We had hit the jackpot. We were on the edge of the stage, just off-camera, at the 1992 Emmy Awards at the Pasadena Civic Center in Los Angeles. The adrenaline was pumping through my veins and I knew Steve was just as excited. Taking a deep breath to calm myself, I looked over at Steve, who gave me a nervous smirk.

Our spot onstage felt like the Grand Central Station of celebrities. Everyone who won or presented an award, or who performed that night, had to stop and stand idly next to us. The presenters and performers

Bret with Disney CEO Michael Eisner

waited patiently for five to ten minutes for their turn onstage. Although we felt a little conspicuous, it was the perfect spot to meet celebrities. Except for the stars, there were only four people in this area: the makeup artist, the stage manager, Steve, and me. Using our best poker faces, we acted as if we belonged, and no one questioned us all night.

In less than an hour we had lengthy and surprisingly interesting conversations with Roseanne and Tom Arnold, Dennis Miller, Burt Reynolds, Kirstie Alley, Jerry Seinfeld, Jane Fonda, Ted Turner, and Cindy Crawford. Steve and I began to discuss the best place to have our pictures taken with the celebrities since there was no photography allowed where we were. That's when Richard Lewis walked up.

As a big fan of Richard, I had always wanted to meet him. He seemed extremely nervous and jumpy, which I found strange, considering he had done stand-up comedy for years and must have done hundreds of live shows. Since opening lines are crucial and determine how a celebrity will view you, I tried to come up with a winner. A good opening line will spark some interest from the celebrity; a bad line will ruin any chance of a good conversation. (When Steve and I met the rock star Meat Loaf a few years back, I opened with "Should I call you Meat, or Mr. Loaf?" He was not amused, although we were.) I quickly ruled out anything regarding Richard's televi-

Steve hanging out with media mogul Ted Turner and fitness buff Jane
Fonda

sion show, *Anything But Love*, since it had recently been canceled.
Steve noticed Richard was wearing a small "Clinton for President"
button, and asked him if he was a big supporter of then-Democratic
presidential nominee Bill Clinton. When Richard smiled and said he
was, the three of us were off and running in a political discussion.
After a few minutes, Richard thanked us for helping him momen-
tarily forget his problems. I asked what was up and he told us, "In
eight minutes, my career will be over."

Richard had been chosen that evening to present a tribute to long-
running television shows that had recently ended: the *Cosby Show,*
the *Tonight Show Starring Johnny Carson, Night Court, Growing
Pains*, and his own show, *Anything But Love*. He said his problem
began when he started collecting clips of the shows to present in the
tribute. All of the shows except his own sent in material, which is
standard in the industry since it's free publicity. His show's producers had refused, for reasons unknown to Richard, so Richard told us
he had decided he was going to go onstage and condemn his show's
production company and producers for their lack of judgment. He
believed that by offending these people he would lose any chance of
working again, but he felt something had to be said for principle's

Bret with John Ritter

sake. While I felt a certain empathy for him, I couldn't help but wonder if the world might not go on for him.

At that point John Ritter walked up with Markie Post, and the five of us continued this conversation. Steve, John, and I offered Richard words of encouragement and he began to relax a bit. Finally it was his turn onstage, and out he went. His performance was great. He explained the situation to the nationwide audience and presented the tribute. Although he criticized his show's bosses, he did it in a way that was funny, getting his point across without seeming spiteful and clearly without damaging his career—quite the opposite, I would say. As he walked off-stage he smiled and said, "Thanks, guys." And indeed, the world kept spinning.

We followed Richard out of the stage area and to the press building, a short walk away. We were still talking with him as we passed a canvas wall that had been set up for this event. All of a sudden an arm reached out through a seam in the wall and grabbed Richard by the shoulder. Richard turned around and I heard "Richard!" and "Hey, Dave!" Richard then ducked into the makeshift doorway. Steve and I looked at each other and I said, "What the heck, let's go." We slipped through the seam, too, and there was Richard talking to a man with an unmistakable gap between his front teeth—David Letterman.

7

Steve with David Letterman

If we were fans of Richard Lewis, we were disciples of David Letterman. What an opportunity: Not only is Letterman my absolute favorite television celebrity, but he's a man rarely, if ever, seen outside of his television show. Dave was the last star I would expect to see at the Emmys in L.A. We joined the group—as peers—and just sort of hung out for a while. We then took pictures with Dave, Richard, and Dave's entourage, including the fascinating Larry "Bud" Melman. I couldn't believe that I was just a pace away from the dental gap I had so long viewed on television. It was quite a night.

# The Jacksons' Victory Tour

The fact that the concert by Michael Jackson and his four brothers at Dodger Stadium in the mid-eighties was anything but exciting didn't stop us from wanting to get close to the band. However, fifty thousand others wanted to do the same, so we knew the odds weren't with us.

The band had just left the stage and the crowd was cheering for an encore. Steve and I shook ourselves out of the trance (boredom) the performance had us in and went to the parking lot to find the Jacksons' waiting motorcade. We had been told by a limousine driver before the show that the Jacksons were not traveling in limousines, but rather in five dark vans.

We hopped into Steve's car and drove around the stadium's parking lot looking for the vans. We hadn't been searching long when we saw four gray vans near a service entrance to the stadium. With three motorcycle police officers parked next to the vans, we were sure we had found the Jacksons' vehicles.

For nearly half an hour we just waited, keeping an eye on the exit and the vans, trying not to look like we were there for what we were there for. Suddenly there was a great commotion, and people began pouring into the vans. Since it was too late for us to run over and meet the Jacksons, we decided to tail the vans. As the four vans pulled out, we dodged traffic to keep up with them. Actually, we nearly caused numerous accidents and just missed flattening hundreds of fans to keep the vans in sight.

We followed the motorcade onto the freeway and were traveling along, laughing, nervous and excited, when suddenly someone behind us started honking his horn and flashing his brights—the car couldn't have been more than six inches from our back bumper. We pulled one lane to the left and slowed down. The vehicle that was bothering us pulled up right beside us, behind the four-van convoy, and we laughed when we realized it wasn't a car, but a fifth van, identical to the first four.

We pulled in behind the fifth van and followed a little way back. After another five minutes the motorcade exited the freeway and continued on surface streets through downtown Los Angeles. The vans pulled up to an employee entrance of the Los Angeles Hilton, and the steel-bar garage door rose. The vans entered and we sped through right behind them. Did we think they had no rearview mirrors? Did we think they might not be aware of fan adoration? But let's get something straight—we didn't adore them. We just wanted to meet them.

At this point we felt pretty conspicuous. Steve said, "If anyone asks, we'll tell them we're with the band and we've got Michael hidden in our trunk." Steve was joking, of course, and the truth was that neither of us knew what we'd say if we were confronted.

We all traveled down a couple of levels into the underground parking garage, and the vans pulled into a parking area adjacent to a hotel service entrance. We parked about twenty spaces down from them and waited in our car to see what would happen. People began pouring out of four of the vans—bodyguards, managers, and finally the Jacksons. We recognized four of the Jackson brothers, but Michael was nowhere in sight.

And Michael was the point—he is the alien. He's the Big Star. He's the challenge. The fifth van was still and hadn't opened. Once everyone else went inside, the driver's door of the fifth van opened. We recognized the man who got out as Marlon Brando's son, Miko, Michael's personal bodyguard. He came over to our car and said, "Can I help you guys?" We couldn't tell him we had Michael in the trunk, because he had Michael in the van—and it was a ridiculous excuse anyway. Steve said, in his coolest, calmest voice, "Nah, we're just waiting for someone." At this, Miko became agitated and said, "Well, he's not coming. Get out of here!" Groping for a way to stay, and to pacify Miko, befriend him even, Steve courted his pity, saying, "I'm not sure how to leave." Miko yelled, "The same @%$#* way you got in!" We left quickly.

We got out to the street and parked. Our previously exciting nervous energy was beginning to turn sour, but we knew the Jacksons were inside and hoped we would get lucky by going inside. So we did.

There were a lot of people in the bar area as we walked in. When we got to the bar itself, we realized we had stumbled into a great party—in honor of the Jacksons. Members of the rock band Journey were there, as were Tom Petty and Quincy Jones; James Garner and radio personality Rick Dees were chatting; and many other celebrities were also there. We talked for a while, calmly mingling with the famous. The food was pretty good, but the bar lacked cranberry juice. The shrimp was decent. Being big shrimp aficionados, Steve and I always judge an event on a 1 to 5 scale by the shrimp they serve. This shrimp was a 3.

As the evening wore on, we decided we'd get to the point and try to find the Jacksons. We hopped into the hotel elevator and pressed every button, hoping that on one of the floors we would see something that might tip us off. When we got to the fourteenth floor, the elevator door opened and in front of us was a large desk with two security agents behind it. One of the agents said, "Turn around and beat it, boys."

We went back to the lobby to think of a plan. Not coming up with much, after twenty minutes we decided to try again. Why not? We were there and we knew where Michael Jackson was. We got on the elevator and pressed 14. To our surprise, the elevator stopped at 3, and in walked LaToya, Janet, Mrs. Jackson, and two bodyguards. Janet was not as famous as she is now, and LaToya was the one with a current album. Steve and I introduced ourselves and began talking about this and that, and we actually broke the ice with LaToya, who started telling us about some of her upcoming projects. The elevator opened on the fourteenth floor and we all got out. Security did not stop us this time—we were with the Jacksons.

We talked for a while longer in the hall, and although we were told that Michael had already gone to sleep, we had a great time. After taking pictures with everyone, we went back to the lobby and rejoined the party. It was a successful night. Sure, Michael's the alien, but we did hang out with some pretty cool, neat people that night, and we knew we would eventually meet Michael later in our celebrity-mingling career.

This event happened to us very early on. As we became more creative and developed the methods you will read about in this book, we began meeting the celebrities backstage at the concerts. Instead of trying to follow a motorcade or waiting for celebrities to leave via the stage door, we were on the inside, eating good food, keeping warm, and most of all, meeting the stars.

## Sylvester Stallone

Whenever you get the opportunity to see a major film star in person, you've got to jump at the chance. When the celebrity is one of your heroes, one of your favorite movie stars, you really have to take a flying leap. Early one morning, I heard a news report that Sylvester Stallone was in town to host the groundbreaking of his new restaurant, Planet Hollywood. Steve and I had recently been to the Planet Hollywood in New York, but weren't able to meet Stallone there. Now, in a few hours, he was going to be in our own backyard, in Costa Mesa.

We immediately got busy utilizing some of the tricks you will learn later in the book, and, in no time, were able to get ourselves on the press list for the groundbreaking. Three hours later, we arrived at the location and were treated to an unbelievable lunch, which, by the way, included some terrific shrimp (4 out of 5 on the shrimp scale). In addition to lunch, we were given free T-shirts and press kits. We learned

Bret talking with Michael Jackson

that the only people at this event were potential big-money investors and the media.

After lunch we were taken by bus to the other side of the shopping complex, where a small stage and microphone had been set up outside an old, closed-down restaurant. We noticed a security guard blocking the restaurant door and figured that was where Stallone was. Walking up to the door as if we belonged there, we tried to walk right through, but were stopped by the guard. He said no one was allowed in, so we went back to the stage area and waited.

In a few minutes, the mayor of Costa Mesa went to the microphone, introduced the project, and then introduced Stallone, who came out of the restaurant. Sly gave a humorous speech and then posed for pictures in front of a prop, the original Darth Vader costume from Star Wars, that was to be used in the new restaurant.

As Stallone turned to go back into the restaurant, Steve and I decided to join his entourage. We mingled with Stallone, the mayor, the bodyguards, and managers, and somehow walked right past the very same security guard at the door. I guess if you just look like you belong, your chances are that much better. Even the mayor probably felt a bit awestruck by Stallone. It was a matter of taking the initiative, or maybe, more simply, of having the guts to try. Or maybe it was just luck.

Bret with Sylvester "I'm not doing a *Rhinestone* sequel" Stallone

Once inside, it became obvious there was no party going on there. The place was just an old, worn-out restaurant, and the only people inside were the ten we had walked in with. No one asked us who we were. Once you're in, you're accepted—the others assume that if you're in, you belong. I figured I might not get another chance to meet Stallone, so Steve and I began to walk toward him. Just then, he turned and walked out the back door of the restaurant with his little group. We quickly followed.

Stallone walked through the outdoor shopping complex to the private restaurant where we had just had our lunch. People walking by noticed that it was Sylvester Stallone and looked like they had just seen a ghost. Folks were leaning out of stores and yelling, "Hey, Rocky!" We just stayed close.

Stallone went into the restaurant, and we followed right behind. We were pleasantly surprised that our passes allowed us into this party. We ended up in the dining room with Stallone and the group of investors. We wasted no time and went straight over to him. We completely dropped the "press" attitude and quickly put on our best "investor" look. So Steve and I calmly chatted with Sylvester Stallone. He obviously could tell we didn't really belong in the investor meeting, but rather than being perturbed by our wasting his time, he seemed interested in our conversation. When I eventually told him we weren't even press, just two guys who were determined to meet him, he almost died laughing. He was a great guy—very funny. We took some pictures with him and wished him luck with his new venture.

# Johnny Carson

We had arrived in London only hours earlier to see Live Aid, the biggest rock concert since the first Woodstock. It was the first time out of the United States for both of us. The concert was scheduled for the next day, so we decided to spend the day trying to find celebrities who were in London for the show. We spoke with several limousine drivers we had run into and were told that a few of the stars were staying at the MayFair Hotel in London. We were also told that Bruce Springsteen, who was staying at that hotel, was driving a purple Jaguar. We had never met Springsteen, and decided it was about time we did. We went to the hotel and waited out front, keeping an eye out just in case a purple Jaguar should appear.

The wait was becoming long and tedious, so we went inside and passed the time talking with some of the hotel patrons who were lounging in the lobby. We were speaking to one couple about nothing special when we mentioned that we were in town for Live Aid. The woman, who was much older than the typical concertgoer, said she was in town for the same reason. We spoke for a while longer, and the conversation turned to Live Aid tickets. When we said we had none and were going to try to get them the next day at the event, the incredible happened—she offered us two prime concert seats. We accepted, of course, and asked how she had come by them. She said, "I got them from my son, Bruce Springsteen." We were pleasantly shocked. After a few minutes of further conversation, Bruce's mother excused herself and said she would see us at the show. We thanked her far too many times and said goodbye.

As Steve and I were leaving the lobby with major smiles on our faces, up drove a purple Jaguar. This was too easy—it had to be our lucky day. We ran out to the curb and waited for the passenger in

Steve trying to book Bret and himself on the *Tonight* show with Johnny Carson

the Jaguar to get out. When the door opened, we were in for a shock. It wasn't Bruce Springsteen at all, but Johnny Carson. We immediately approached Johnny and started talking. Steve asked him if he was in town for Live Aid, and Carson said no, he was in London for the Wimbledon tennis tournament.

Johnny seemed very happy to talk to a couple of guys from his home state. Incidentally, none of the other folks hanging around the area had any idea who Carson was. One woman observing the scene later asked us, "Why were you so excited? Who was that?" Steve told her he was only the most famous television host in America. She was still not convinced that we should be so excited, but we were. We talked with Johnny for at least twenty minutes. As we left, we raised our hats to the former King of Late Night. There were no shrimp served in front of the hotel, but we did meet Johnny Carson; and it was well worth killing half the day for this achievement. Carson, incidentally, was not nearly as stale as his show was in its elderly years.

There was a very high luck rating on this one, but it shows that one thing can lead to another. If you go out there and try, and if you look like you belong, and if you learn some of the tricks in this book, you'll be able to create the very same luck we had.

# 3

## *Getting Started*

**I**t is helpful in beginning your own career of meeting celebrities to develop and improve your telephone manner. The telephone will become your key instrument in obtaining invitations to the important events. When you make your calls you need to feel confident and you need to present yourself as if you deserve to be on the guest list.

To help get your feet wet, this chapter will show you how to use the telephone to obtain free entertainment merchandise, and by doing so, you will learn the various important telephone mannerisms needed to accomplish your ultimate goal.

We will concentrate on obtaining free CDs, press kits, and tickets. You know what CDs and tickets are, but let's take a minute to explain press kits. A press kit is a marketing package created to give members of the press information about a particular product. We are interested in the products of movies and music.

In the music industry, the record companies have departments that are set up specifically to deal with the press. These departments are typically called publicity or press relations. A publicity department will develop a press kit to help drum up media interest in a new CD release. The press kit will contain a variety of items, including a description of the new CD, biographical information on band members, 8x10 glossy publicity photos, bumper stickers, novelty items, and even the CD itself. These kits are sent out to members of the

Bret and Steve enjoyed a Sting concert for free, courtesy of Sting's record company's generous publicity department

press in the hope that the reporters will then write a review or article about the new release.

In the movie industry it is the same. Publicity departments at the film companies create press kits to help sell movies to critics and other members of the press. Each press kit contains descriptions of the movie and its stars, color and black-and-white pictures, and novelty items. I've also seen movie press kits that contained shirts, movie passes, toys, watches, and a myriad of other items.

To obtain a free press kit, you have to call the publicity office of the company releasing the movie or CD and ask for one. It is really that simple. The only question the publicity department will ask you is what press organization you are working for. Anticipating that question, before you call any publicity departments, you must first make a quick call to your local newspaper.

Every community has a local paper, and you need to find the smallest paper possible. If your community has a guy producing a weekly four-page newsletter out of his garage, perfect. If the smallest paper is the equivalent of the *New York Times*, that will work also; however, it is quicker and easier to gain your "press affiliation" with a smaller outfit. Here's how it is done.

Bret with Academy Award–winner Tom Hanks and model Jill Bennett

Call your local paper and ask to speak with an editor. You will probably be transferred to an assistant, especially if you call a rather large paper. It really doesn't matter who answers your call—even a secretary will do. Explain to the newspaper employee that you have an interest in writing for their paper and would just like a chance to submit your work. Tell them you will submit the work for free. If they like it, they can publish it; if they don't like it, they can throw it away. The employee will give you a name and address for submitting your article. A paper will always say yes to your request. Steve and I have done this hundreds of times, and the newspapers have never said no. We have spoken with some very small newspapers and with huge papers like the *Los Angeles Times*. The paper has nothing to lose. If you submit a piece that would make the most seasoned reporter proud, they can print it. If you submit a lousy article, they will merely disregard it. Either way, the paper has no problem. And you have a legitimate story to tell the publicity departments of the various movie and record companies that you choose to contact.

So you have called the *Kalamazoo Weekly Reporter*, and they have told you to go ahead and submit an article; they'll take a look at it. You are now ready to call publicity departments and get free mer-

Bret with Michael Keaton just before the release of the first Batman movie.

chandise. For example, let's say you just saw Michael Keaton's movie, *The Paper*. You loved the film and have always been a big fan of Keaton's work.

To get the press kit for the movie, you have to find out which movie company to call. Simply look at the movie's ad in the newspaper and find the name of the movie company in the credits at the bottom of the ad. For *The Paper* the movie company is Universal Pictures. Call directory assistance in Los Angeles (213-555-1212) and ask for Universal Pictures. Almost all of the film and record companies are based in Los Angeles, so this is a good place to start.

The operator will usually give you the phone number and location of the film company, even if it is located in a different Southern California area code (310, 818, 714, 909, 805). In this particular case, the operator will tell you that Universal Pictures is located in Universal City, in the 818 area code, and give you the number. You are now ready to make your call. Your conversation with Universal will go something like this:

UNIVERSAL:  Universal, how may I direct your call?

YOU:  Publicity, please.

UNIVERSAL: Is that publicity for feature films or television?

YOU: Feature films, please.

UNIVERSAL: Domestic or international?

YOU: Domestic, thanks.

*(The phone call is then transferred.)*

UNIVERSAL: Good morning, publicity. How can I help you?

YOU: Yes, I was calling to receive the press kit for your movie *The Paper*.

UNIVERSAL: Are you with the press?

YOU: I am writing a review of the movie for the *Kalamazoo Reporter*.

*(Never lie. You always want to represent yourself truthfully. In this case, you are writing a review for the* Kalamazoo Reporter. *Whether they print it or not is another story.)*

UNIVERSAL: Great, did you get a chance to see the movie yet?

YOU: Not yet. I wanted to wait to get the press kit first.

UNIVERSAL: No problem, you're going to love the movie, it's fantastic. Let me just get your information. What's your name and address?

Publicity departments are in business to help the press. They love it when you call. They want to send out press kits, so you are doing them a favor by accepting one. When you phone, you'll get the feeling that they can't do enough for you.

You will be nervous when you make your first call. Don't worry about it. It's very easy, and the people answering your call want to help you. If you make a mistake, like somehow insult the actors or the film to the publicity person, the worst that will happen is they won't send you the press kit. But don't worry, there are thousands of publicity departments around, and you'll do better the next time.

Furthermore, the publicity department you just had a problem with won't remember you in two months, so you can even call back there when their next film that you are interested in comes out.

Be sure to call for publicity kits when the movie or record first appears. Usually the first week of release, or before, is the best time to call. It is fun to get the press kit for a major movie that isn't even released yet. For example, showing your friends the press pictures of Sylvester Stallone in *Judge Dredd* a week before it is released will amaze them, and make you the center of attention. When you first see ads for a new movie coming out, that's a good time to phone.

The process works the same way for press kits from record companies. The record companies, however, have more to offer you. The publicity departments at the record companies can send you the actual CD, or even concert tickets. The trick is, you have to ask. If you call for a press kit, they will send you one, but that's all they'll send you. Ask for a copy of the CD and tell them it will help your review. They will usually honor this request only during the first week of release—not before and not after. If you want to go to the group's concert, and they are touring in support of a new CD, call the publicity department and tell them you want to review the live show. You will not only get to attend for free, but usually you'll be given some terrific seats.

The best example of how well this can work happened to Steve and me over ten years ago. In the early 1980s, Billy Squier was our favorite musician. We had gone to his concert at the Long Beach Arena and had gone backstage, where we met Billy, Olivia Newton-John, Sheena Easton, and a few other celebrities. Just by coincidence, we had brought along one of Olivia's record covers. We didn't know she would be there, but had just grabbed a couple of covers to use as paper for autographs.

When we met Olivia, she kept asking us how we knew she was going to be there—our explanation that the record cover was a coincidence was not believable to her. But we took some pictures and got a few autographs, and had a great time.

The next day we decided to try to get free tickets to the next Billy Squier show, at Irvine Meadows, which was scheduled for the following day. I called the publicity department at Capitol Records in Hollywood, since that was Billy Squier's record label at the time. They told me tickets for the press were no problem and to come down to the record company to pick them up, because the concert was the next day and the mail wouldn't arrive in time.

When I got to Capitol the next day, I was in for a big surprise. I went up to the publicity offices and when I walked in, ZAMBO, Billy

Steve with Billy Ray Cyrus—another free concert.

Squier was there! He had stopped in to take care of some business. I told him how much I enjoyed the show the night before, and then he asked me if I was the one who had had the Olivia Newton-John record covers. When I told him it was me, he said, "I got in some serious trouble with my girlfriend because of you guys!" I asked, "Why would that be?" He said, "Only my girlfriend and I knew Olivia was coming to the show, so my girlfriend was sure I told you guys." I assured him it really was a coincidence that we had the record covers, and we laughed about it. He then asked me if I worked for Capitol, and I suddenly remembered why I was there. I turned to the publicity person and told her that, actually, I was there to pick up the publicity tickets to Billy's show I had arranged with her earlier. She handed me two tickets, but before I could look at them, Billy asked to see them. I handed the tickets to Billy, he looked them over, and then handed them back to the publicity person, saying, "Give him some real tickets."

The publicity person then handed me two third-row seats for the concert. I thanked everyone and told Billy I would see him the next night. The concert was great—Def Leppard was the opening band. David Lee Roth came out and sang with Billy Squier during an encore, and Steve and I had a terrific time.

Bret with James Woods

An interesting result of this experience was that the publicity person at Capitol became a valuable contact. She remembered my meeting with Billy Squier, and for years after—until she left Capitol—she would give Steve and me almost anything we wanted when we called for tickets, press kits, or CDs. She had seen me talking to Billy Squier and figured I was important.

Most people you meet during your search for celebrities are just as interested in the famous and celebrated as you are. The very same publicity people who control the tickets and CDs at the big companies love celebrities. These PR types are usually the biggest star-chasers of them all—that's why they go after these jobs in the first place. They might not admit it, but offer one of them the opportunity to meet one of her idols and watch her jump at the chance. Use this to your advantage. If you can ever help her meet stars, or if you give her pictures of entertainers she's interested in, she will do favors for you in the future. As you begin to build relationships with people who are connected, you will begin to meet more and more stars. Contacts are very important.

# Establishing Contacts

**C**ontacts are critical for meeting celebrities. It is also important to keep in mind that everyone you meet along the way is a contact. Tell all of your friends and acquaintances that you enjoy meeting celebrities and would like any introductions they can make. Tell them you will, of course, reciprocate.

Once you start a photo collection of yourself with the famous, show it off. People get very excited when you show them these pictures. They love to hear stories about stars and will always ask you how you met them. Find out what your friends and acquaintances do and see how that could fit into your plans. A florist might make a delivery to a celebrity's home one day; a gas station attendant might fill up a limo with gas—and find out that the passenger is going to a big Hollywood party; or a busboy could be working at a restaurant that becomes a celebrity hangout.

Make contacts, and lots of them. Contacts will be very helpful in getting you invited to big events, as well as vital to finding celebrities.

The first big celebrity Steve and I met was Elton John. Elton was receiving the key to the city of Los Angeles in the early 1980s. The older brother of a friend of ours from school was a maintenance worker at City Hall and heard about the event. When he called home to tell

Steve with the legendary Bob Hope

his brother about Elton's impending arrival, Steve and I were there. We all decided to rush down to City Hall and see the spectacle.

When we arrived, we were surprised to find a low-key atmosphere. There were no marching bands playing or huge crowds waving PIN-BALL WIZARD signs. There were at most five other people. Elton arrived with two bodyguards and a minimum of fanfare. After a very brief ceremony, Elton stopped and signed our *Goodbye Yellow Brick Road* album cover and posed for pictures.

We couldn't believe that we were standing next to a man who had sold out stadiums around the world and had *owned* the music charts for the last ten years. We were excited for the rest of the day, but by next week in school we had almost forgotten about it. Then we got the pictures back. The following day we showed them to a few friends at school, and by the end of the day everyone was asking to see the pictures, including the school newspaper teacher—who wrote an article about us. We became instant celebrities at school. For weeks, people we had never met were coming up to us and asking about Elton John, and, what's more important, chicks began to dig us. We decided we couldn't come up with a better, or more enjoyable, way

Bret with the legendary Elton John

to meet girls than by meeting additional celebrities and document-ing these occasions with photos of ourselves with the celebs.

The key to this story is that anyone can be a contact. We met Elton John because we knew a janitor—actually, we knew the brother of one. However, we were very lucky in this case. Usually you won't get any celebrity information from contacts unless the contact knows you're interested. In the seventies and early eighties everyone was interested in Elton John, and we happened to be around when the call came in. But remember to tell everyone about your celebrity pur-suits. They will help you, especially if you can help them. And believe me, our phones ring off the hook with daily tips.

There are some specific places you can look to make contacts. Cer-tain professions lend themselves to celebrity contact:

# Limousine Drivers

When celebrities go out, whether in Hollywood, New York, Miami, or anywhere in-between, they usually take a limo. You will see excep-tions, but a limo is the norm. Most limo drivers work for a limou-sine company and not for a particular celebrity. They drive many types of people, from teenagers on prom night to a couple on their first date to Paul McCartney or Madonna. The drivers know who will be in their car and where they are going, so they can offer you valuable information. Limo drivers make about $10 an hour plus tips and usually are not trying to build a career around driving, so they are not worried about giving out whatever information they may have. Therefore, they are excellent sources. They can tell you when stars are coming into the airport, or to which restaurant they are going, or in which hotel they are staying.

Meeting limo drivers is quite easy. One way is to get a few of your friends together and each pitch in about $20. You can take a limo to a concert, dinner, school dance, or anywhere else, for that matter. Treat the driver like a friend, not like a servant. Include him in your conversation and invite him to your function. Most of the time they will decline, but they are always appreciative of your offer. Toward the end of the evening, after you have become somewhat friendly, ask him what celebrities he has driven. Limo drivers, just like everyone else, are interested in the famous and will gladly tell you stories about famous people they have driven. When you explain that you go to a lot of celebrity events and meet a lot of famous people, the driver will be interested. Usually you can offer to take him to the next celebrity event you are planning to attend in return for him giving you a call the next time he runs across interesting scheduling information about someone famous.

If you're not interested in spending any money, you don't have to pay for a limo to meet a driver. If you see a limo parked in front of a restaurant or hotel, stop and talk to the driver. They are usually bored, just waiting next to their cars for hours and hours while their clients are inside. The driver will usually be happy to talk to you; it gives him something to do.

In 1992, Steve and I were at a radio station watching a few members of the rock group Queen do an interview show called *Rockline*. We had been invited by a sound engineer we had met at the Grammy Awards the year before. We went outside to get a breath of fresh air and struck up a conversation with Queen guitarist Brian May's limo driver. The driver asked us if we knew where the Atlas Bar and Grill was. We gave him directions and then asked him if that was where Brian May was going after the radio interview. He said he wasn't sure, but there was a big party for Sting there.

A limo driver told Bret and Steve he was driving Dudley Moore

Once the interview ended, we talked with the members of Queen for a bit and then rushed over to check out what was happening at the Atlas Bar and Grill. A huge party given by Sting's record label was underway. We had no trouble getting in because there was no security at the door. They figured anyone who knew about the unadvertised party must have been invited by someone. It was a terrific night—the shrimps were a 3 on the shrimp scale—and we met a slew of celebrities: Bruce Springsteen, Sting, Michael Keaton, Billy Idol, and Jeff Bridges, among others.

Once again, a newly made contact offered us valuable information. You just have to ask. The man who was Brian May's driver that night has turned into a great source of information for us over the years. We even took him to the American Music Awards show that first year. He drove us in the limo for free and has been calling us ever since with celebrity sightings and party information.

Limo drivers are terrific; help them meet celebrities and they will do the same for you. It is one of the few perks in their otherwise boring job.

Bret with rocker Billy Idol at Sting's party

## *Hotel Workers*

If your best friend is the general manager of a famous Beverly Hills hotel, then you obviously have a major-league contact. However, most of us are not that lucky. Steve and I do have friends who are bartenders, bellhops, and room service workers at many of the famous Los Angeles and New York hotels. It is easy to make these contacts.

First of all, you can hang out in the hotel's bar for an evening. You'd be amazed at how good a friend you can make of the bartender after a couple of hours of conversation. Keep in mind that although you might go to the hotel to make a contact, these people are *people*—don't expect to just use them. Not only would that be unethical, but it probably wouldn't work. Most people are smart enough to spot a phony. Be sincere, you can be friendly without being a phony. Make sure you are willing to offer as much to the relationship as you expect to get from it.

If you want the bartender or room-service worker to call you when a celebrity checks in, you must be willing to take them along to an event or reciprocate in some other way. Steve, who sells washers and dryers for a living, once got a great deal on a washer-dryer set

Steve with *Stripes, Meatballs, Caddyshack,* and *Ghostbusters* star Bill Murray.

for a valet we had met at the Beverly Hilton. The valet was so thankful that he has been calling us for over two years now, every time a celebrity checks into that hotel. One hand washes the other.

## Restaurant Workers

Restaurant workers are the same as hotel workers. There are certain restaurants in every town that have great reputations for food, or are known as celebrity hangouts. Eat there and get to know the people who usually get no attention, like the busboys. A busboy at a famous restaurant like Spago can be just as valuable as a maitre d', if the busboy is willing to call you when a celebrity arrives.

Additionally, the busboy is much more approachable than the maitre d', or the famous chef in the kitchen. Imagine trying to gain access to Wolfgang Puck, the celebrity owner-chef of Spago, as opposed to Joe Smith, who is clearing the tables. There is no contest. Choose the easiest path; you'll get the same info.

Steve talking with Bruce Springsteen over dinner

## *Anyone Backstage*

Our motto is, "If they're backstage now, they can get *us* backstage next time." When you go backstage—and you will be able to do that after you read the next few chapters—introduce yourself to anyone who will listen. Pass out your business card and collect as many cards as you can in return. Everyone backstage has contacts. They might be famous themselves, they might work for someone famous, they might work for a company related to the entertainment business, or they might just have some influential friends.

As you talk with people you might hear about parties later that night, or about a famous producer who is looking for a new washer-and-dryer set for his house (or something else you can do for him because of your job or contacts), or about where the shrimp have been set up. Every conversation can help you. It might help you that night or in the future, but it will help you. It was the sound engineer we met at the Grammys who invited us to the Queen radio interview. We had talked with him for a half an hour between the Grammy rehearsal and the live show. He told us he was hungry but couldn't leave his station, so we got him a sandwich and a drink. He was thankful, and that small gesture really broke the ice. He has invited us to a few celebrity events, and we have been playing softball with him on Sundays ever since. You'll find that food can be a great tool in developing a lasting contact. And don't be snobby about meeting the hired help. Some of these folks are well connected, and they make good money, too.

# Security

If ever there was a group of people interested in food, it is security people. Most of the security personnel at major events seem to be former high school and college football players. They are six-foot-four and weigh around three-hundred pounds. Their job for the evening is to guard a door, or equipment, or a specific celebrity. Most of the time they stand in one place for four to five hours, without a break. When you come along, being friendly and offering them a break from the monotony of standing around doing nothing, they are often appreciative. Work an offer of food into the conversation, and they will jump at the chance. Then, just like the lion who gets the thorn pulled out of his paw, the security guard becomes your friend for life. If you want to go through the door now, go right ahead. If you want to bring ten of your closest friends, what does he care? He's making $5 an hour and you gave him food. He will do what he can within his power to help you out.

The best example of this happened at the Grammy Awards in 1993. Steve and I were determined to meet Michael Jackson. He was one of the few major stars with whom we had not been photographed. We were talking to a photographer from *Rolling Stone* magazine, and he told us we had no chance of meeting Michael—he wouldn't pose for pictures with anyone. The photographer then told us that Michael would be going straight from his dressing-room trailer to the stage and back. We went over to Jackson's trailer and saw that it was being guarded like Fort Knox. We began talking with a security guard we had never met before, who was standing at attention outside Michael Jackson's trailer. He was a nice guy, but emphatically said that there was no way we were going to meet Michael. We changed the sub-

Steve with the King of Pop—Michael Jackson

ject and starting talking to him about the Superbowl. His interest level increased, and five minutes later, he mentioned how long he had been just standing there, and how he was looking forward to the end of his shift so he could rest his "howling dogs" and get a bite to eat. ZAMBO. We had him.

Steve made a beeline to the greenroom, where food had been set up for the entertainers, talent, and invited guests. I kept the conversation going for a few minutes until Steve returned with roast beef and turkey sandwiches and two Cokes. Starting a conversation we've used with many security guards, Steve said to me, "Which sandwich do you want?" I answered, "I'm not hungry." Then turning to our soon-to-be-good-friend, security guard Phil, I said, "You said you were hungry, why don't you take my sandwich?" Steve said, "Here, Phil, pick your favorite."

Not more than five minutes later, Phil told us that if we waited around for another half-hour he would get us in to see Michael. Phil came through and we had a good time meeting Michael—all because of the kindly guard who we treated right.

# Publicity

You learned in the last chapter how to get press kits by calling record and movie company publicity departments. Remember, it's possible to use these people as contacts also. When a music group comes to town, it is the publicity department of the record company that will manage the backstage party, including the guest list. If you are friendly with someone in that department, your name can easily be put on the list. Even if you've only spoken with the publicity person once, when you called for a press kit, call back and act like you're best friends. Thank him for the press kit and tell him you would like to go to the concert, get backstage, if possible. Most of the time he will remember you, and if he doesn't, that can work to your advantage also. His job is to cultivate relationships. If he has forgotten you, he might pretend to remember you and add your name to the guest list just to avoid the embarrassment, or he might be apologetic about forgetting your previous conversation and add your name while repeating, "I'm sorry."

It's amazing how long you can work a negative situation, like when they forget you, into a positive one. If the publicity agent has forgotten you and you use that to your advantage, the agent will definitely remember you next time and will bend over backward to help you, trying to prove that he or she hasn't forgotten again.

# Members of the Press

The press is invited to virtually all celebrity events. The more press people you can meet and associate with, the better. Offer to help them cover a story. They'll oblige, if for no other reason than that you will be good company. Meet up with press people at the events and strike up conversations. You can make a good many important contacts just by meeting members of the press.

# Anyone Else

Always remember, anyone can be a contact. Some of our best contacts are not included in any of the above groups. Our very best contact works as a baggage handler at the airport. He calls us whenever

Bret with John (*Full House*) Stamos

a celebrity is flying into town. If it is someone we're interested in, we will go to the airport and wait by the gate. There you will usually bump into a limo driver who is carrying a sign with the name of the celebrity. We will start talking with the driver and the flow of contacts continues. We will not only meet the celebrity, but we will find out what he is in town for: a big event, a special party, whatever. Then we will work—or, more accurately, network—our way toward getting invited to all of those events. Don't ever underestimate your ability to befriend a famous person, or at least a member of her entourage. The excitement never ends.

# Obtaining Credentials

**O**ne of the best tools you can obtain to help you meet celebrities is a press credential. A press credential will give you instant credibility and will open a lot of doors for you. The best part is, they are not difficult to get. You just need to ask in the right way. The process is very similar to what we covered in chapter 3, when we discussed how to get press kits. You need to establish some affiliation with a news agency, whether it be a newspaper, radio station, or magazine. This is not hard to do.

Let's assume that you want to visit the set where Harrison Ford is filming his latest movie. The quickest way to obtain a press credential is to call the lowest-circulation newspaper in your hometown, let's call it the *Daily Reporter*, and tell the editor you are a freelance writer going to the movie set and would like to submit an article about your experience. Even if the editor is not the least bit interested in your story concept, he will tell you to go ahead and submit it. It is easier for the editor to say that than it is for him to say no.

No one likes to say to no. It makes most people uncomfortable. An editor will tell you to submit the article, if only to pacify you. The article could surprise him by actually being good, and he will print it, but at the time of your inquiry, he figures saying yes to your request is an easy way to get you off the phone.

As far as you are concerned, however, once the editor says yes, you are legitimately writing for that paper. Your next call will be to

Bret with Harrison Ford on the set of *Clear and Present Danger*

the film company producing Harrison Ford's movie. Tell the publicity agent that you are writing an article for the *Daily Reporter* and would like to visit the set. You aren't lying—you are writing the article. Whether the *Daily Reporter* prints it or not is not your concern. Any good publicity agent will jump at the chance to have the press go to the set. As I mentioned earlier, publicity agents are in place to help the press. The more press coverage a publicity agent can generate, the better she is doing her job. You will be given a time and date to visit the set. It's as easy as that. They actually want you to visit!

This system works for many types of events and with many types of media. For instance, you can use the same strategy and call a national magazine, like *People* or *Rolling Stone*. Just remember when you call the magazine, stress that you just want to submit your work—you don't expect anything. You're not asking for money or a promise they will publish your piece, just a chance to submit it.

Another method of obtaining press credentials is through radio stations. All radio stations, whether Top forty, talk radio, news, country, or whatever, are interested in celebrities in one way or another. Call your local station and tell them you can get celebrities to make

Bret with the Thin White Duke—David Bowie

custom station IDs. Station IDs, like "You're listening to the Wackerman Brothers on KLOX 97.6 FM, Los Angeles," are required by the Federal Communications Commission (FCC) to be played at least once an hour on every radio station. Since the stations are doing them anyway, they love to spice them up in some way—and celebrities certainly can do that. Custom celebrity station IDs, like "Hi, this is David Bowie, and you are listening to those crazy Wackerman Brothers on KLOX 97.6 FM, Los Angeles," are in high demand by radio stations. And anyone can get them.

The station's only hesitation would be the amount of money you might charge. Tell the station that you would like to prove the quality of your service and will give them the first few for free. No station will turn down the possibility of free celebrity station IDs. Make sure to stress to the station that you are not offering celebrity impersonations, but the actual celebrity. Once the station says yes to your service, it is time to call the event of your choice. Tell the event the station you are working for, and ask for your press credential. It's a sure thing.

Always remember to follow through on your promises, however. If you are at an event using the radio station method, make sure to

Bret with classic crooner Tony Bennett

get some radio station IDs. Bring any type of tape recorder with you. An expensive DAT tape recorder will provide better sound quality, but a cheap $25 cassette recorder will do just fine. Some of our best station IDs have been done on my daughter Brittney's My First Sony tape recorder. The celebrities think the recorder is funny, and it helps get them to do a funny ID. Don't be shy about approaching a celebrity for an ID, they do them all the time. Every time they do an interview on TV or radio, the station will ask for an ID. At the big events like the American Music Awards or Grammys, the radio and television station reporters are always asking for IDs, and the celebrities are almost always happy to oblige. It is a normal part of business for them. You can write down the ID ahead of time so the celebrity won't have to invent one himself, or just tell him the station call letters (KLOX) and let him ad-lib. Either way, it works. We have prewritten some pretty funny ones. We had Tony Bennett say, "Whenever I'm rocking out, I listen to KLOX—pure rock." It was so out of character for Tony Bennett that the ID turned out great.

We have also had some great IDs ad-libbed by celebrities. Portly George Wendt, Norm of *Cheers* fame, said, "Whenever I'm working out, my headphones are tuned to KLOX 97.6 FM."

Steve with George "Norm" Wendt

Just relax and act like you do IDs all the time, because the celebrities do. Of course, after your event, submit your tape to the station quickly. The station will no doubt be thrilled with the IDs, and probably will be willing to offer you some type of payment the next time you call.

Also follow through if you use the newspaper method. Write an article and submit it to the newspaper. If you've never written before, read some other articles of the same type and do your best to write a similar one. If you went to a concert, look at past concert reviews in the paper. If you went to the Golden Globe Awards, go to the library and see how other papers covered them last year. Write the best article you can, and you might get lucky and have it published. Newspapers are very interested in celebrities, because the public is always interested in them. If your story is appealing, they will use it. You may even create a good career in journalism by using this method.

Steve and I have sold numerous articles over the years, and have been offered employment ranging from an entry-level staff reporter's job to a weekly celebrity gossip column. If we had been interested in reporting as a career, we probably could have done quite well.

Steve with Burt Reynolds and Loni Anderson at their last major public appearance before their breakup

If you are happy with your current career, but would like to also pursue journalism, you can make a good living working as a freelance reporter. A freelance reporter is not on the payroll of a newspaper or magazine, but instead is paid for published articles. If you are submitting articles that get printed, you can begin to negotiate fees and create a second career for yourself. The benefit of being a freelance reporter is that you don't have to be at the newspaper from nine to five. As a freelance reporter you are your own boss and can keep your "day job." The negative side is you only get paid when a newspaper wants your article. In any case, you're meeting celebrities and having a great time. Additionally, if you are "pen-a-phobic," like Steve, get yourself a partner who likes to write. Or hire your brother for $5 an article. Just make sure you submit something.

Another method for establishing credentials is photography. You contact the newspapers or magazines in the same manner, tell them you are going to an event, and ask them if you can submit pictures. Steve and I use this method quite often. We take pictures at the event anyway, and it is faster to send copies of the pictures to the magazines, newspapers, and tabloids than it is to write an article. This method can also be profitable. Magazines and tabloids will pay about $500 for any picture they use. The price can escalate quickly if you take a picture of something newsworthy, like a major star and his date, who turns out not to be his wife, or turns out to be his new girlfriend.

Careers in journalism and photography and radio IDs aside, even if you never see a single one of your efforts published, you are still making contacts with every phone call, you are still building your credibility with publicity agents and those people who control the guest lists, and you are still getting into all of the great events.

# Finding
# Celebrities

**Y**ou can't meet celebrities unless you know where they are. Obviously, when you go to the Grammy Awards or the Academy Awards, you will meet a lot of stars. However, if you know where your favorite movie star is eating lunch the next day, or if you know that your favorite musician is going to a certain tennis exhibition, you can meet that particular person. Every month you see pictures of celebrities arriving at airports or dining in restaurants in magazines like *People* and *Entertainment Weekly*. This chapter will explain how the paparazzi know where the celebrities are, and how you can use that same information for your own purposes.

Finding celebrities outside of special events is not difficult. Everywhere a celebrity goes, people usually notice, even if the star is trying to "dress down." If you have built up a good network of contacts, you will be called. When the celebrity leaves his house, he will probably get into a limousine. If the limo driver is a contact, you're in business. When a star arrives at a restaurant, you will get a call if you know somebody there. You will get a call any time a celebrity goes anywhere, if you have a contact in the right place. That is why making contacts everywhere is important. Make contacts at gyms, antique stores, record stores, donut shops—everywhere. You would not believe how many times Steve and I have heard from a celebrity, "How did you know I was going to be here?"

Bret and Steve with a big piece of Americana—Don Knotts

Last year we got a call from a contact who worked at a real estate office. The contact told us that Don Knotts, of Barney Fife and Ralph Furly fame, had just come into the office and had gone with an agent to look at some property. As far as Steve and I are concerned, Don Knotts is the greatest actor who ever lived. Not only did he create the ultimate lawman, Barney Fife, on the *Andy Griffith Show*, but he invented fashion as the resident manager on *Three's Company*. And those accomplishments pale when compared to some of his feature-film work: He was *The Incredible Mr. Limpid*, he was *The Love God*, and who can forget his memorable performance in *The Apple Dumpling Gang*?

We went straight to Steve's garage, where we have erected a shrine to Don Knotts, and grabbed some classic publicity photos. Our next stop was twenty miles away—the real estate office. We arrived well before Mr. Knotts returned from property-hunting and waited patiently. About an hour later, he arrived. He was bigger than life. We were looking straight into the eyes of the man who had stared down many a criminal in Mayberry. He is a legend. We gathered our emotions long enough to start an intelligent conversation with him, and we soon discovered that he was by far the nicest, most sincere, hippest celebrity we had ever met. When we showed him the publicity photos of his younger exploits he seemed shocked. He said, "I decided to come down here about two hours ago. How did you know I was coming here?" He couldn't believe that not only had we found him, but we had his publicity photos with us. We had a great time with Don and took a few pictures with him. It took Steve and me over a week to calm down after our incredible meeting.

I realize that Don Knotts might not seem as important in the "celebrity world" as Michael Jackson, or Sylvester Stallone, or Heather Locklear, but we had grown up with Don Knotts. Everyone has that one star they want to meet. It doesn't have to be the biggest name in the entertainment industry, but someone you have really enjoyed, or someone you really respect. Don Knotts was *it* for us. That was a great day. You can also have your great days by putting our proven techniques to work.

You can see how important every contact can be. When you begin your celebrity-meeting career, you might overlook potential contacts. A real estate office receptionist isn't the most likely celebrity locator. However, when you add the real estate office receptionist to a list of hundreds of others, it is difficult for a celebrity to go anywhere without coming in contact with one of your connections.

Quite frequently, when a celebrity is going out for some reason, a handler will call ahead to make some type of arrangements—a table at a restaurant, seats at a ballgame, a limousine for transportation. This practice makes the star's activities go more smoothly, and it also makes your job of meeting her easier. When the handler makes arrangements ahead of time, it allows you more time to gather the tools of your trade: camera and film, tape recorders, special items for autographs, etc. It also allows you more time for travel to the star's location and for other preparation, like making sure the car has gas. As an example, I received a call earlier this year from a contact who worked as a limousine dispatcher. He told me that he had just scheduled a limousine pickup for tennis great Andre Agassi for a run to the airport. He told me what time the limo was picking up Agassi and what time he would arrive at the airport, as well as airline and gate information. Luckily, the limo was scheduled to get Agassi to the airport in about three hours, which gave Steve and me plenty of time. I called Steve and we decided to meet back at my house to pick

Bret with tennis great Andre Agassi

up a tennis racket for Agassi to sign. We then went to the airport, and Agassi arrived like clockwork. He was alone in the limo and, after we got the conversation going in our patented, proven way, we all sat down in the airport lounge and Agassi treated us to cranberry juice and fried shrimp. (Normally we are against frying any type of crustacean, but it was free, so what the heck.) We spoke with Agassi about everything from tennis to Barbra Streisand. Celebrities are normal people and can relate to nonfamous people like you and us.

When we asked Andre to sign the racket we had brought, he laughed and said he was wondering why we had brought it. We told him that we had come down to the airport just to meet him. He got a big kick out of the racket. If we had not gotten the advance notice, we wouldn't have had time to run home and get the racket, and Steve and I always like to bring some type of unusual item that might get a rise out of the celebrity we are going to meet. We had the old publicity photos to show Don Knotts and a tennis racket for Agassi— which was a little unusual in the middle of the airport. If you don't own anything that has something to do with the celebrity, just bring any unusual item. We once had John Travolta sign a pair of boxer shorts. If you ask politely, they will do whatever you ask!

Bret with *Pulp Fiction*'s John Travolta and his wife, Kelly Preston

We have had numerous actors sign rolls of toilet paper we'd bought at local convenience stores minutes before we met them. We have even had musicians sign brooms. (Everyone has picked up a broom and used it as an air guitar at one time or another.) Any unusual item, whether it be a tennis ball or a yo-yo, will make a celebrity laugh, and that will start off the conversation. They are besieged by autograph hunters pushing pens and paper in their faces, so you should strive to be different.

There are other ways to find celebrities besides waiting for the phone to ring. If you are interested in a particular star, call his management company and ask what he is doing that week. It is part of the management company's job to schedule the celebrity's time. If you don't know the particular celebrity's management firm, call the last place you know the celebrity worked. For instance, if you were trying to find Vince Neil, the former lead singer of Motley Crüe, you would call Motley Crüe's record label. To find out the label, just look on any of the band's tapes or CDs. The label's office personnel will tell you that Vince is no longer with the band and that you need to direct all inquires to his management company. Then they would give you the number.

Bret explaining to Sharon Stone that he is married and she'll have to find somebody else

If you were trying to find actress Sharon Stone, you could go to the video store and look at the video box of her latest release. It will list the movie studio that produced the picture. When you call the movie studio, ask for publicity, and then ask the publicity agent for Sharon's management company. They have no problem giving you that information. The same works for television stars—call the television network that carries the program (ABC, CBS, NBC, Fox, et al). Remember, those who are shy are lost.

Once you have the management company's name and number, give them a call. Ask them what project the star is currently working on. You'll be surprised at how much information they will give you. Not only will you learn about upcoming projects, you will find out when and where movies are being filmed; or what studio a particular musician is recording in and what nights he is recording; and almost anything else you might be interested in. Get the name of the person you talked to and make sure to leave your name—remember, you're always making contacts.

Steve with Ace Ventura: Pet Detective—Jim Carrey

You now know where and when a star is going to work. Go there at the right time and usually you will have no problem meeting her. It is the old theory: If you are there, you must belong. Remember, however, that the star is there to work. Don't be a pest; she's got a job to do. But if you're patient, you will get the chance to chat with the star during breaks and at other opportune moments.

# 7

## The Big Events

**S**o far in this book we have seen how to develop your telephone skills by requesting free press kits, concert tickets, and CDs. We have showed how to make important contacts, and lots of them. We have explained how to obtain press credentials from your local newspaper. All of these techniques have gotten you primed for the big time.

This chapter will outline the big secrets that will allow you to meet any celebrity. We will discuss using the tricks from the previous chapters, plus a few important new ones, to gain invites to all of the really major events.

### Award Shows

- Academy Awards (movies)
- Emmy Awards (television)
- People's Choice Awards (television, movies, music)
- Grammy Awards (music)
- Country Music Awards (music)
- Soap Opera Awards (daytime television)
- MTV Awards (music)
- MTV Movie Awards (movies)
- Golden Globes (television, movies)
- Tony Awards (theater)

- ESPY Awards (sports)
- American Music Awards (music)
- American Comedy Awards (television, movies, stand-up)
- American Television Awards (television)
- Billboard Music Awards (music)
- Soul Train Awards (music)
- NAACP Image Awards (movies, television, music)
- Comedy Hall of Fame (comedy)
- Rock and Roll Hall of Fame (music)

## Other Special Events

- Superbowl
- World Series
- Concerts
- Film shoots on movie sets

This list is just a sampling. New awards shows and special events are added every year. Tribute concerts and celebrity roasts are scheduled constantly. You just have to keep your eyes open.

A good place to keep up-to-date on celebrity events is in the "Life" section of *USA Today*. As awards shows are approaching or new events are scheduled, *USA Today* gives a short report on when and where the show will appear, as well as a list of celebrities scheduled to attend. Other sources are entertainment industry trade papers like *Variety*, the *Hollywood Reporter*, *Billboard*, and *Radio & Records*. Your local paper also will carry some of the regional information in its "Entertainment" or "Show" section.

I noticed a small article in the *Los Angeles Times*'s "Calendar" section about the opening of Andrew Lloyd Webber's new play. The list of expected attendees was incredible. Steve and I went and met everyone from Bob Newhart to Darryl Hannah to Clint Eastwood.

Do a little homework, read the papers, and write down the events as you notice them. If you don't write down the events in some sort of calendar to remind yourself, you will end up reading about how great the event was in *People* magazine. Also, write down the list of expected attendees. This will help you watch out for specific stars while you are at the event.

Steve backstage helping the Red Hot Chili Peppers with their Grammy Award

As you begin to use the tricks in this book and go to these events, you should fine-tune these techniques to your particular style. Some of the people we have taught to go to events prefer to use only telephone techniques, while others prefer to use only contacts, and still others use a mix of all of the possibilities. You will also find that not every method will work for every event—but one of them is sure to be successful. Steve and I have not been "shut out" of an event in over ten years. Every method that follows has been tested, used over and over, and will definitely work for you, too!

## *The Opening Band Theory*

It only makes sense that if you called Barbra Streisand's management and asked for an interview at her upcoming concert, your odds of being granted the passes you want are slim at best. However, if you called and requested an interview with the bass player in her band, your odds are closer to a sure thing. Since your ultimate goal is to attend the concert and meet Barbra, do you really care who gives you the backstage passes?

The bass player is probably just as interested in fame and publicity as anyone else, but you can guess how many journalists are beat-

Steve with his favorite psychologist-cartoonist, Bob Newhart

ing down his door: not many. He will most likely jump at the opportunity and try to help you out as much as possible.

After you receive the passes, don't forget to follow through with the interview. It is not only the ethical thing to do, but you are again cultivating a powerful contact. The bass player has access to Barbra Streisand and the after-parties, and will probably go on to play for other big names in the future, once the Streisand tour is completed.

This technique works well. You can almost always use this method with success. The one tool you do need is some affiliation with a press agency. But have no fear. As chapter 5 pointed out, gaining the affiliation is not difficult. This method also works in a variety of situations. For instance, if you want to meet Candice Bergen, of *Murphy Brown* fame, instead of trying to get an interview with Candice, call and request an interview with Joe Regalbutto, who plays investigative reporter Frank Fontana on the show.

Tell Joe you would like to interview him on the set. You will not only have great fun talking with Joe, but you will also meet Candice. As another example, to meet the members of Guns 'N' Roses while they are on tour, call the management company of their opening band and set up a meeting with them.

Steve with *Murphy Brown* regular Joe Regalbutto

This method even works for major awards shows. If you want to go to the Grammy Awards, call one of the bands that is up for Best New Artist, Duo, or Group. Since this category recognizes new talent, these bands are still enjoying their new-found success. Choose a band that most people feel has no chance to win—they will usually be more accessible. Tell the band's management that you want to do a story on the band that culminates with their nervousness over the award. You have to be there to chronicle the events. This method has worked for well over one hundred awards shows for Steve and me, as well as for people we have trained.

## Super Intern

For any given awards show there are well over one hundred people and organizations working the event. Each one of these offers you an opportunity to gain access. The entertainment industry is a business. The companies working the event, from lighting to catering, are trying to make money. They pay for supplies and employees, and charge the event a fee. You can personally increase the profits of any one of these companies by offering to become an employee—for free.

Steve with Guns 'n' Roses lead singer Axl Rose

Choose any firm that is working the event and offer your services on a volunteer basis. The beauty of this is that you don't have to have any skills whatsoever. You call the company and tell them that you are interested in their line of work, and would like to intern for them to "learn the ropes." It is difficult for the guy on the other end of the phone to turn down your free offer. He knows the show is hectic and that an extra worker will make things that much easier—he only wishes there were ten of you making this offer. You are not expected to come in with any talents or knowledge—you have already told him you want to intern to learn the business. The company will use you, and you will have fun learning some backstage skills. And, when showtime nears, things do become very hectic, and you are usually left alone since the regular crew is too busy to teach you anything. As a result, you are free to goof off and walk around backstage and meet any celebrity you want, with your valuable all-access credentials.

This method has a positive benefit in addition to your main goal of meeting celebrities that evening. Every person you work with during your "internship" can become a contact. These people have passes to awards show after awards show. If you become friends with them, they can and will give you passes in the future. At the very

Bret with the Fresh Prince of Bel-Air, Will Smith

least, they can give you information as to where the after-parties are and where the big stars are going. These details are crucial if you are to have a good time after the event.

The following is a sample list of jobs that were performed at the last Grammy awards. You can become an intern for any of the people or firms that are handling these positions.

| | |
|---|---|
| Executive Producer | Associate Director (2) |
| Producers (2) | Associate Director/Editor |
| Director | Segment Producer |
| Executive in Charge of Production | Pre-Telecast Producer |
| Coordinating Producer | Staging Coordinator |
| Production Executive | Production Manager |
| Writers (3) | Talent Coordinator (3) |
| Production Designer | Seating Coordinator |
| Lighting Designer | Talent Escort Coordinator |
| Musical Director | Talent Flow Coordinator |
| Sound Designer | Talent Assistants (3) |
| Sound Consultant | Talent Assistant–Dressing Rooms |
| Script Supervisor | Pre-Telecast Coordinator |

Pre-Telecast Public Address
  Announcer
Art Director
Music Contractor
Costume Designer
Wardrobe
Choreographer
Script Coordinator (2)
Chyron P.A.
Stage Managers (8)
Music Equipment
Security
Announcer
Makeup Supervisor
Makeup (5)
Hair (5)
Assistants (3)
Production Coordinator
Credentials
Production Associates (6)
Secretarial
Legal
Technical Director
Video Control (2)
Videotape Operator (2)
Gaffer
Board Op
Camera Operators (8)
Steadicam
Focus Puller
Chyron
Electronic Graphics
Backtimer
Audio Mixer (3)
Audio Maintenance
Public Address Mixers (3)
Monitor Mixers (2)
Utility (7)
Sweetener
Audio Facilities
Audio-Video

Catering
Closed Captioning
Computer Rental
Editing Facilities
Fax Machine Rental
Furniture Rental
Hotels
Insurance
Limousine Service
Monitors
Music Clearance
Office Supplies
PA System
Parking
Payroll Services
Electrical
Public Relations
Remote Camera
Telephone Operations
TelePrompTer
Tent Rental
Travel Agencies
Tuxedos
Typewriter Rental
Video Facilities
Walkie Talkies
Xerox
American Federation of
  Television and Radio Artists
  Union (AFTRA)
American Federation of Musicians
  Union (AF of M)
Directors Guild of America (DGA)
Writers Guild of America (WGA)
National Academy of Recording
  Arts and Sciences (NARAS)
NARAS legal
Awards Supervisor
Nominee Telecast Seating
Promotional Ticket Seating
Press Room Security

Nominee Reception
Requests for Invitations
Accounting
Press
Program Book
Photographer

Television Committee
Television Network
TV Sales
TV Business Affairs
TV Promotion

## The Three-Phone Call System

For most events, you can secure yourself an invitation just by asking for it. The trick is to ask the right people in just the right way. To be successful with this method you must be confident on the phone and must have developed a good telephone manner. That is why chapter 3, "Getting Started", was so important. There, you were taught how to make calls to publicity offices and request press kits. The conversations you had during that process are key to preparing you for this chapter. You have to feel comfortable on the phone, and you have to come across as if there is no doubt in your mind that you should be on the guest list.

The first phone call you will make is to the event itself. The people putting on the event open production offices at the venue and have telephones installed about a week before the event. To get the number, call the venue's general offices (not the box office). As an example, if you wanted to go to the Grammys, you would call Radio City Music Hall's general office number. You don't want to call the box office because they won't be of any help. Your conversation with the general office should go something like this:

RADIO CITY: Good morning, Radio City. May I help you?

YOU: I need the number for the Grammy's production office on-site.

RADIO CITY: Surely, it's (212) 247-4777.

Obviously, your first phone call is not difficult. It is short and to the point.

Your next phone call is to the Grammy's production office. Here you are going to ask for an invitation to the event, but don't expect to get one on this call. You are merely gathering information for call number three. You are trying to find out who is in charge of the guest

Bret discussing with Eddie Van Halen and John "Cliff Clavin" Ratzenberger the possibility of starting a new band, "Van Clavin"

lists, the name of the person you are speaking with, and her title and responsibilities. To get that information, your call should mimic the following:

GRAMMY:   Grammy production, can I help you?

YOU:   I would like to speak with someone about guest credentials.

GRAMMY:   Credentials for the press, crew, or just attending invites?

YOU:   Attending invitees, please.

GRAMMY:   That would be Louie Yankowitz; he's our production coordinator and he's in charge of that list.

YOU:   Great, I appreciate your help. What was your name?

GRAMMY:   No problem. My name is Sarah. Glad I could help.

(*The phone call is then transferred.*)

LOUIE:   Lou. What can I do for you?

YOU:   Yeah, Lou, I was told to talk to you about being added to the guest list.

LOUIE:  Oh, no, I can't add anyone to the list, I'm just in charge of confirming the invited guests and making sure they get their passes.

YOU:  Okay, who should I call to be added?

LOUIE:  You need to talk to Jim Calder over at Legas and Legas, they're handling the Grammy's public relations.

YOU:  What's the number over there?

*(While he is checking for the number, use this "dead time" to try and get more information by using intelligent small talk.)*

YOU:  Things must be pretty hectic around there right now, with the show getting so close.

LOUIE:  It's crazy.

*(They say that everytime. No matter what show you are calling about, or whom you are talking to, they always feel that they are overworked and that things are going nuts, so, it's a good question to open him up for a little small talk.)*

YOU:  Do you handle anything else for the Grammys beside credentials?

LOUIE:  I'm the liaison for the television network. I make sure they have everything they need, here on-site.

YOU:  Wow, that must keep you busy.

Louie will give you the number of the public relations firm. The information you now have is the public relations firm's name and number, a contact at the firm, and Louie's name, title, and responsibilities. It is time to make call number three. This time you will actually be added to the list, so be confident. Pick up the phone and call the public relations firm. Note that Louie might have given you a different contact name, like someone at the television network or some other place, but the key is that he gave you the name of the person in charge of adding people to the guest list.

Your call to the public relations firm is actually easier than the call to the production office. It should go like this:

PR FIRM:  Legas and Legas.

YOU:  May I speak with Jim Calder, please?

Bret with Phil Collins

| PR FIRM: | May I tell him who's calling? |
|---|---|
| YOU: | Bret Saxon. I was referred to Jim by Louie Yankowitz over at the Grammys. |
| JIM: | Hi, Bret, what can I do for you? |
| YOU: | Louie told me to get in touch with you about adding my name to your guest list. He said I needed to call you since you're the big guy. Louie says things are nuts over at Radio City, so you guys must be just as swamped. |

By throwing in the hectic line again, you not only put yourself on a conversational level with Jim, but you have sped up the process. Jim, agreeing that his world is hectic, will now skip over any questions he might have asked you, and will just add your name.

Make sure to ask him to add your name, plus one. You probably don't want to go to an event by yourself and "plus one" is standard industry jargon. You wouldn't say, "Put me down for two, I want to bring a friend." Even if you want to bring four other people, merely say "plus four." Keep in mind, however, that the more invitations you request, the more likely they are to question your affiliations and get suspicious.

Bret with real estate tycoon Donald Trump, before his "assistant," Norma I. Foerderer, turned us down for a shot of Trump for the cover of this book

As soon as the receptionist announces your call to Jim, he assumes that you are someone in the industry since you already know Louie. Again, it's the old theory that if you are there, you must belong. You know Jim's name, you know Louie, you know things are hectic for him, so you must belong on his guest list.

## Service Broker

This method plays on two important concepts: first, that the events themselves are businesses, and as such are open to business deals that benefit them by saving them money; second, that most people love to be associated in some way with the entertainment business. What we have done, very successfully, is combine these two concepts. Steve and I will call the production offices of an approaching event and speak to one of the production coordinators. We will offer the show some free service, such as flowers to decorate the dressing rooms, press rooms, backstage area, greenroom, or even the production offices. We tell the coordinator that we will supply this service completely free of charge. Our only request is four all-access passes to the event. The coordinators love this offer. If it is a ser-

Bret discussing current affairs (and Bret's book) with Walter Cronkite

vice, such as a Xerox machine, that they were going to rent anyway, your offer saves them money. If you offer a service they were not planning to spend money on, they still will like the offer if they can see a benefit for themselves.

Some services Steve and I have supplied in the past include: flowers, computers, tuxedos, catering, and printing services.

The other step in this method is to find a business that will supply the service you are supposed to provide—for free. You can find a business first and then approach the show, but we have found it easier to approach the show first. You can feel out the production coordinator for a service they can utilize. If you recruit a particular business first, and then the coordinator tells you that they are already under contract for the Xerox machine, or that the producer is allergic to flowers and won't allow any at the location, you've wasted your time and you're out of business.

You will have no problem finding a business to donate its goods in return for two of the backstage passes. Almost everyone we have ever approached has bent over backwards trying to talk *us* into using *them*. A owner of a tuxedo shop or restaurant, for instance, is initially excited at just the prospect of working the event and being

Steve with his teenage crush, Brooke Shields

around stars. Then he begins to realize that it is also a good business decision. He can begin to advertise that he has supplied catering services or tuxedos to stars. If you are savvy and use your imagination, the business owners will line up to give away these services.

As the broker, you will be getting this business together with the event. You are the deal-maker, the Donald Trump of this very unique field. Once the deal is made, the business will do everything. You end up doing no work, just enjoying the benefits of attending the event with your guests, for free, with all-access passes!

## House Photographer

Similar to the service broker method, is offering yourself as the house photographer for the event. The production office will probably tell you that the press will cover the event just fine. That's when you tell them your unique angle: You will cover the event, for free, using a behind-the-scenes approach. Whereas the press will be shooting pictures only of stars entering the event, or in the press room, you will be shooting everything behind the scenes. You will take pictures of the celebrities preparing to go onstage, of the sound crew

Steve giving Garth Brooks a tip on a good cowboy-hat sale

working behind their soundboard, of the hair stylist working on the stars. . . .

Depending on who you are talking to, include his job as an example of what you will be shooting. Make him understand that he will be in pictures with the stars. Just because a person is working the event doesn't mean that he isn't interested in celebrities. Quite the opposite, actually. Play on that. He will want these photos to show his family and friends.

## Seat Fillers

At every televised event, from awards shows to tributes, there is a need to keep every seat filled to create the atmosphere of a standing-room-only crowd. The producers want to make sure the television audience believes that the show is so popular and entertaining that there isn't an empty seat in the house. Since this is generally not true in reality, people are actually hired to fill vacant seats left by no-shows, people who leave early, or even people who just get up to go to the bathroom. The show will hire from 150 to 200 people to fill those seats. This method not only gets you into the event, but

Steve and Carly Simon just outside the press room at the Grammys

you get the best seats—up front, next to the stars—and sometimes you are even paid for the evening.

To become a seat filler, call the event at least a week or two before. Ask the production office for the company or person in charge of seat fillers. You will be given the number and then you just call and offer your services. They will invite you down for an interview. The seat filler companies are always looking for dependable people, and you will have no trouble being hired if you dress nicely and show up to your appointment on time.

## Press

At the big events, press rooms are set up. One room is for the print media, where the stars will take turns standing on a small stage and answering questions asked by the journalists. Another room is for media photographers, where the stars will take turns standing on another small stage while photographers shoot hundreds of pictures in two minutes. Other small interview rooms are set up for television shows, like *Entertainment Tonight, E! News Daily, Extra,* as well as for the various networks.

Bret with former heavyweight boxing champ Evander Holyfield

After a star presents or wins an award or performs onstage, he or she is escorted to each of these press rooms. As the evening goes on, a backlog builds up outside the press rooms. This is a good place to meet celebrities, since they are stuck there until they are asked to go into the room for photos or interviews. While the members of Van Halen are being interviewed in the first press room, Garth Brooks may be waiting outside for his turn. This is a good opportunity to spend five to ten minutes getting to know a celebrity.

To be invited to the press rooms, simply follow the methods laid out in chapter 3. As explained there, call your local newspaper and ask if you can submit a story about the upcoming event. Once they give you the OK, call the event and ask for press credentials. They will ask what newspaper you are with and then add you to their press list.

## Contacts

As I have emphasized throughout this book, contacts can get you any-where, including to the big events. Everyone you meet at an event can be a contact for the next event. If you have made a good contact, don't be afraid to call and ask for passes to an upcoming event. You won't get the passes unless you try, and you have nothing to lose.

Try to think of some service you can offer your contacts in return for the passes, or simply ask for a favor. This is a business of "what comes around goes around," and your contact will be calling you for something in the future. Some contacts who can really help you get into the big events include security personnel, publicity agents, sound engineers, stage managers, event producers, etc. Make your contacts and then utilize them for all they're worth. Remember, if you are shy, you will lose out on some valuable opportunities.

# *Etiquette*

So you've used all the tricks and methods in this book, and you're looking across the room at Don Johnson, David Bowie, or Sylvester Stallone. Now what do you do? It's your moment of truth. This chapter will tell you what to say to get the conversation started, as well as give you a few dos and don'ts to keep in mind when meeting celebrities. This is a crucial chapter that will help you in social situations for the rest of your life. You will learn just what to say to someone you really want to meet.

The first thing to keep in mind is that celebrities get approached by fans, admirers, and lunatics everywhere they go, all around the world. The stars are experts at signing a quick autograph and moving on, usually as quickly as possible, to get away from fans. But Steve and I aren't interested in a quick autograph or picture. We enjoy meeting the celebrity and spending some time talking, whenever possible. The problem is, you can't just walk up to a star and say, "I was hoping to monopolize a lot more of your time than you're used to and, if that's all right, I want to be your buddy at this event." If the star perceives you as a "fan," he might be very cordial, but he will try to move on as soon as possible, which is what stars are programmed to do. They don't spend too much time with any one admiring fan.

The trick is to find a way to get the star interested in what you have to say. If you walk up to a celebrity and say anything like "I just love your show, you're the greatest," your conversation is over. The

Steve using a great line to start a conversation with former Beatle George Harrison

star will thank you and walk quickly away. They hear compliments all day long and are very jaded. You might be very sincere when you tell Anthony Hopkins how great he was in *Silence of the Lambs*, but he has heard it thousands of times. He almost expects everyone to say it. Additionally, if you tried to be different by telling him he was stale and unconvincing as Hannibal Lechter, he probably would be offended and your conversation would certainly be over. The idea is to say something unusual that will get a laugh, or compliment him in a way he is not used to, or get him talking about a subject he is interested in that's outside of the entertainment industry.

One of the best ways to get a conversation going is to do some homework. Know who is going to be at the event you are going to and then find out some nonentertainment facts about the star.

When Steve and I met action hero Steven Seagal at the premiere of *Under Siege*, our first question was if he missed his old days as a Howling Coyote at Buena Park High School, his alma mater. I can say pretty confidently that there wasn't another person at the premiere who knew what high school Seagal had gone to, except maybe his mother. His reaction was great. We immediately put ourselves on a different level than that of fan. He started reminiscing about how

Steve with Michael J. Fox

it seemed like a lifetime ago, and we traded old high school stories. We became his buddies, confidants, and old friends because we were original and had done our homework.

As another example, when Steve and I met Michael J. Fox, we started talking about hockey and asked him who he thought was going to win the Stanley Cup that year. We were guessing he would be interested since he grew up in Canada, and, sure enough, we pressed the right buttons. Toward the end of our conversation, Michael said, "Hey, it was nice talking to you guys. I get sick of all of this Hollywood bullsh*t. Don't forget to put your money on Montreal." This was the ultimate compliment for us. We had succeeded in drawing him out of his celebrity shell.

If you have done your homework and know some aspect of the star's life, you have the best topic for your opening line to the celebrity you wish to approach.

The second time Steve and I met Sylvester Stallone, we started out the conversation by asking him when he was going to do a sequel of *Rhinestone*. He said, "God forbid, not in this lifetime." Because it was a question he had probably never heard before, we were immediately past the fan-meeting-a-celebrity problem.

Steve and Bret with "Stuttering" John Melendez

Just remember to be different. Catch the celebrity off-guard. You probably don't want to go too far, like Howard Stern's celebrity interviewer Stuttering John. Stuttering John asks questions meant to embarrass or tick off his subjects. The reactions Stuttering John gets out of the stars are often hilarious and make for terrific radio and TV, but won't endear him to the celebrities. But you've got to give the guy credit, he gets the job done and his questions are original.

As I have said, if you have done your homework and know some aspect of the star's life, you have your best topic for your intelligent opening gambit. Chapter 10 provides a celebrity index that will give you facts about many of today's biggest stars. Use the index to find interesting topics to help you with an opening line.

If you don't know anything about the star, ask a question he wouldn't expect. We had a lot of success last year at the American Music Awards asking celebrities who they were picking to win the Superbowl. Everyone had an opinion, and our conversations worked very well.

When asking for a picture with a celebrity, you should have had a conversation with her for at least a few minutes beforehand. Once you have used a good opening line and then engage in a conversation, it is easy to ask for a quick picture. Steve and I always wait

Bret with *Tonight* show host Jay Leno

until the end of the conversation to ask for pictures. When the conversation has gone well, the celebrity is much more "into" taking a picture with you, and will look at the camera and smile.

We brought a friend with us to the ESPY Awards last year, and he wasn't interested in listening to our sage advice about techniques for talking to celebrities effectively. He would walk up to celebrities, interrupt their conversations, and ask for pictures with them as if he deserved their time and effort. Most of them quickly said no, and the pictures of the ones who agreed turned out to be terrible. The stars were looking the wrong way, or upset, and obviously completely uninterested. Your pictures will come out much better, and the celebrities will be more agreeable, if you use the techniques laid out in this chapter.

Another aspect of etiquette at star-studded events concerns food. As far as food is concerned, just don't be a pig. If you want to eat fifty to sixty shrimps, as Steve and I will do at any given function, make ten discreet trips to the buffet table. You don't want to walk away from the food with a plate piled to the roof, because those celebrities and honchos who happen to observe you with the overloaded plate will immediately assume you have no manners. They

Steve and Van Halen's Sammy Hagar, discussing fashion

will assume you are without class, or a freeloader, or some other negative stereotype that you do not want to project (even though it is probably true).

Regarding attire, the way you dress is really up to you. If you don't like to stand out, wear exactly what is expected. However, the days of everyone wearing a tuxedo for the Grammy Awards are over. At the Grammys there are plenty of men wearing everything from jeans and ripped shirts to Armani suits to the standard tuxedo. About the only event where a tuxedo is expected is the Academy Awards, and even there you see plenty of men wearing business suits. An evening dress is fairly standard for women at most of the events, but you do observe a number of them wearing jeans, spandex, and leather.

Steve and I try to dress appropriately, according to the event's norm. However, to help break the ice with celebrities, we have found that strange, original clothing can be a bonus. When Steve wore a wild red-and-silver jacket to the MTV Awards, we met Sammy Hagar, lead singer for Van Halen, who was wearing a very similar jacket. Sammy actually started the conversation by saying to Steve, "I don't know whose jacket is uglier." Now if only Brooke Shields or Sharon Stone had noticed.

Bret with *Wayne's World* star Dana Carvey

When it comes to etiquette, be creative but not obnoxious. You want to stand out from the normal "fan," but you don't want to identify yourself as a nut by not knowing when to quit. Go to the events and have a good time. You'll get used to meeting the stars, and it will truly become second nature. Stars are actually often relieved when, in the midst of a party with hundreds of strange people, we come over and have a comfortable chat with them.

# Business Opportunities

**W**hile you are out meeting celebrities and impressing your friends and neighbors, there is no reason why you can't make some money along the way and enjoy some free perks as well. Even though meeting celebrities is exciting enough to do for free, there are business opportunities you should be aware of. As far back as Elvis Presley merchandise right up to current advertising trends, celebrities sell. Every year billions of dollars are spent on celebrities, from movies to merchandising to endorsements.

Steve and I have come up with some methods for getting a piece of the action.

## Free Perks

Before I show you how to make yourself rich, I'll explain how you can enjoy free services as a result of your celebrity fun. Two services that are easy to obtain are tuxedos and limousines. As I pointed out in chapter 4, if you have contacts at certain businesses they will give you their services free, in exchange for passes to an event or some other consideration. But even if you don't have a contact anywhere, you can still enjoy services for free.

For free tuxedos: Bring a collection of your pictures of celebrities or, better yet, of you with celebrities, into the shop and tell the owner

Steve with Billy Joel

what you do. Tell the owner you will wear his tuxedo to the next event. Point out that every picture of the stars will include you in the tux. While it might not seem like much, the tux shop owners Steve and I have dealt with jump at the chance to have their tuxedos seen next to stars. If the owner seems a little reluctant, tell him you will hold up a small sign that says TUXEDOS FURNISHED BY BILL'S TUXEDOS. He'll see the pictures as a great way to brag to customers and friends about how great his products are.

To get free limousine service: After you show the owner of the company the picture collection of you with stars, tell him that you will pass out his business cards to all of the talent agents, personal managers, executives, and celebrities at the event. Tell him his own employee, the driver, will be able to witness your efforts and confirm that you are delivering on your promise.

Steve and I do not own tuxedos, or limousines, for that matter, but we have attended at least four black-tie events each year for the past six years without ever paying the tux rental costs. Additionally, we take a limousine to almost every event—absolutely free. We do, however, tip the drivers. We're not total cheapskates.

Bret with Hall of Fame baseball player Johnny Bench

# *Restaurant Promotion*

A good way to make money without going out of your way is through restaurant promotion. You do this by obtaining pseudoendorsements from celebrities for a restaurant.

When you go to events, you will probably want to take pictures with the celebrities. To make extra money, you just have to add the logo of a restaurant to the picture. For example, wear a T-shirt or jacket with the name of the restaurant emblazoned across the front, or hold up the restaurant's menu when you take your pictures.

Here's how this concept works: First, go to a restaurant and tell them about the events you go to. Sports bars and pizza places are usually the best bets. Show the owner of the place your pictures of yourself with celebrities and tell him you will hold up his menu when you take pictures at the next major event. The owner will love the idea. Help close the deal by telling him how great it would look for him to hang a picture of his menu with Michael Jordan or Johnny Bench on his wall.

Tell him you could get enough pictures with major celebrities to make an entire "wall of fame" for his restaurant. The owner will be

Bret with hockey legend Wayne Gretzky

excited about the chance to have some affiliation with the stars. It will probably even help his business, in addition to his self-esteem. Then tell him you charge $25 a picture.

At a typical event, Steve and I get about twenty-five pictures each. If you can get half that, you will make about $300. If you go to an event each week, you can make extra income of $15,000 a year, if you are good. If worse comes to worse and the owner doesn't go for the bait, tell him you'll trade the pictures for two or three free meals. He will definitely say yes to this!

## Selling Pictures and Autographs

The autograph business is big right now. Stores that sell only autographs are popping up from local malls to catalogs, and everywhere in-between. Every one of these businesses is looking for autograph sources, and that is where you come in. If you collect autographs at the event, you can turn around and sell them for a substantial profit. Autographs of sports celebrities like Michael Jordan and Wayne Gretzky sell for as high as $400, depending on what the autograph is on.

Bret with Guns 'N' Roses guitarist Slash

A Gretzky autograph on a cocktail napkin is probably only worth about $50, but the same autograph on a hockey stick is worth the full $400. You probably wouldn't want to carry around a hockey stick at an awards show, but a hockey puck can fetch from $100 to $200.

When you get an autograph, create your own proof of authenticity by having the celebrity hold up the autograph while you take a picture. This is important. Steve and I had Slash, guitarist for Guns 'N' Roses, sign a guitar. When we brought the guitar to a guitar shop to sell, the owner told us he would pay $100 for it, which barely covered the value of the guitar. We asked him why a Slash autograph wasn't worth much, and he said, "If I knew it was a real autograph, I would give you a grand, because I can turn and sell it tomorrow for two thousand. But how do I know you guys aren't just good forgers?" We then went to the car and got a picture we had taken of Slash holding the autographed guitar. We went home five minutes later with $1,000. You can do the same thing if you study the advice in this book.

Remember, when getting photos or signatures, always imply that they are for you, your girlfriend, boyfriend, parents, or best friend.

Bret with Jerry Seinfeld

Never, and we mean *never*, let celebrities suspect you're going to sell the stuff, or you will really tick them off. Celebrities get paid big money to endorse things and they don't want people like you or us cutting in on their action.

Selling pictures is a little different. You can sell pictures to magazines, newspapers, local record stores, or gift stores that have celebrity merchandise. These places want interesting photographs of the stars and will usually give you much more if you are not in the pictures. Pictures range drastically in worth, depending on the subject. For instance, the pictures of Princess Fergie topless, sucking on her boyfriend's toes, were sold to the tabloids for hundreds of thousands of dollars. However, if you have a picture of Jerry Seinfeld holding up his Emmy, it is also valuable to a magazine—in the $100 to $500 range.

The easiest sale is to the record stores and gift stores. They will buy a picture from you for around $5 and turn around and sell it for $15. If you want to make more, put the pictures in the store on consignment and split the retail price with the store. The profits can add up because you are not just selling one copy of each picture. A good picture of the teen idols from television's *Beverly Hills 90210* or *Melrose Place* can sell up to one hundred copies to junior high and high

Bret with *Beverly Hills 90210* star Luke Perry

school kids in a local record store, so the money can start to add up. Make sure, however, that you get the store manager to sign a receipt for the photos that clarifies the deal, so they don't try to rip you off later by changing the terms.

## Unsigned Band Promotions

If you are really ambitious, you can help emerging music bands get their first big break. In a business where it is all "who you know," it is difficult to get record company executives to listen to a new band's tape, no matter how good the band is.

The reality of the business is that a record label will receive over ten thousand demo tapes for every band that is actually signed. And the band that is signed probably didn't just mail in the tape; they probably knew someone in the industry.

The beauty of it is that you will know people in the industry when you start going to events like the Grammys. You will be rubbing shoulders not only with celebrities, but also with the power players in the recording industry. You can meet the vice president of Capital Records's A and R department (the department that signs new talent)

Steve with Clint Black and Lisa Hartman

while you're both grabbing for some shrimp in the buffet line. After a short conversation, you can discreetly and shrewdly hand him a band's tape. If your excitement over the band is sincere and your rap is believable, the executive will not want to miss out on a good opportunity, and will listen to it because of your endorsement. You have just increased the band's chances of being signed by 1,000 percent. The band still has to be good, but at least now they will be heard.

Offer to get a band's tape into a record industry executive's hands. Tell the band you will provide this service for free, but if the band gets signed as a result of your efforts, you want 15 percent of their advance. That 15 percent can amount to $5,000 or $10,000. Naturally, you should put this deal in writing and inform the band that it will apply to any company that you can demonstrate you hooked them up with through your efforts with their demo tape.

## Other Opportunities

As I mentioned in chapter 5, a good business opportunity is to record radio station IDs. Once you have developed a relationship with a radio station, you can begin to charge them about $50 for each ID. When you have built up a catalog of around twenty station IDs, you can market your services to stations across the country. You can call the program director or creative services department and tell them about your business. Tell them you are going to send them a tape of some of your work. About a week after you send your tape, follow up with a phone call. Believe us, you will soon have more business than you can handle.

Other business opportunities are available in the media. You can become a journalist by starting out as I outlined in chapter 3. After you have submitted a few articles and they have been published, start lobbying for a position as an entry-level reporter. If the newspaper likes your work, you will have a good shot.

Another possibility is to become a talk show correspondent. While you are backstage at the celebrity events, you will see and hear some interesting things. The talk shows are always looking for "insider celebrity information." It also helps if you are outgoing, funny, and feel comfortable in front of the camera. The first television program Steve and I were featured on was the *Joan Rivers Show*. We were a little nervous while we were waiting for our turn on Joan's couch, but when the lights went on, we both were too busy telling celebrity stories to remember our nervousness. Joan made us feel very comfortable. If you become a regular correspondent, you will be paid fairly well. If you decide to only go on talk shows when you feel like it, you will still enjoy terrific perks. The shows fly you to where they tape (usually New York, Los Angeles, or Chicago), put you up at terrific hotels, and limo you around the city. Sometimes you are paid a nominal fee for your appearance, but it is worth it just for the free vacation.

One method for making money, which I certainly wouldn't condone or recommend, is to get yourself beaten to a pulp by a leading celebrity. We know of a photographer who would insult and ridicule celebrities, trying to coax one of them into attacking him. He was hoping to get punched and then sue the offending celebrity for millions. Everyone has heard of huge out-of-court settlements by Sean Penn, Jack Nicholson, and others to settle suits of this nature. Thankfully, there are thousands of different avenues to make money that

Bret and Steve being featured on the *Joan Rivers Show*

are less painful and more ethical, and you will come up with your own. Steve and I think of new opportunities every time we go to an event. Not all are as profitable as others, but it never hurts to try.

If all else fails, you can make a decent sum of money by writing a book about your adventures. Give me a call. I know a great publisher in New York.

# 10

## Celebrity Index

**W**hen you use the methods outlined in this book, you will find yourself standing face-to-face with the world's most famous personalities. This chapter will help you figure out what to say to them. We have compiled a list of top celebrities; given a brief accounting of some of their most famous work and accomplishments; some small facts that can be used to start conversations with them; and a rating of how easy they are to approach, based on our experiences. For example, if you were standing across the room from Jerry Seinfeld, what would you say to get a conversation started? How nice can you expect him to be? Well, all you need to do is look up Seinfeld in this chapter to find out. Jerry's listing looks like this:

### Jerry Seinfeld

Jerry Seinfeld has become one of the hottest stars on television thanks to his top-rated television sitcom, *Seinfeld*. The show began in 1990, but was consistently beaten in the ratings by *Home Improvement*. Once it was moved in the lineup to follow *Cheers*, it raced up the ratings list to number two. Since then it has been one of the most popular shows on television. Jerry was a very successful stand-up comedian before his role on *Seinfeld*, and, in fact, the character he plays on the show is also a stand-up comedian. A good conversation starter with Jerry would be his short time as Frankie on the sitcom *Benson* during the 1980–1981 season. Jerry was born in New York on April 29, 1957. He is happy to sign autographs and take pictures and genuinely seems down-to-earth. Rating: 8.

You can use this information to see, first of all, that based on our meetings with Jerry, we have given him a rating of 8 out of a possible 10. This means that Jerry is pretty much a great guy and you should have no problem approaching him. Next, you can see that he played a small role on the television sitcom *Benson* way before he hit the big time with *Seinfeld*. You now have a great conversation starter. Jerry gets approached every day and hears "I love your show" or "You're just so funny on Seinfeld." He is tired of hearing it. If you use a line like that, he will automatically categorize you as a fan. Using the information in this chapter, you have a way to separate yourself from the average fan. You could go up to Jerry and say, If there is a *Benson* reunion show, would you participate to give your character Frankie another chance at the big time? You would have just hit him with a question he has probably never heard before. At a minimum, you will get a laugh out of him and will be on your way to a great conversation, autographs, pictures, or whatever you want.

All of the information in this chapter will help you in your conversations. If you happen to be from the same hometown as a celebrity, you now have something in common. If you share a birthday, again, you now have something in common. Find the common ground and use it. Keep in mind that all the information contained here was compiled through personal experience or the research of a lot of our friends. Some of the facts might not be 100 percent accurate. However, we have tried to be as thorough as possible.

## Willie Aames

Willie Aames is best known as one of the stars on the television show *Eight is Enough*. He was born on July 15, 1960, and was raised in Huntington Beach, California. His real name is Willie Upton. A good conversation starter with Willie would be about his childhood in Huntington Beach and hanging out at the Huntington Beach Pier. He

Steve with Paula Abdul and John Stamos before their breakup

also had a band for a while and would play at his old schools and hangouts in Huntington Beach after he became famous. He is very open to autographs and pictures and is very accessible overall. Rating: 8.

## Paula Abdul

Paula Abdul is best known as a Top Forty pop singer. She started out in show business as a Laker Girl. The Laker Girls are the cheerleaders for the professional basketball team, the Los Angeles Lakers. Abdul excelled at dancing and made a name for herself by choreographing music videos. She hit it big with her solo debut album. She later married movie star Emilio Estevez, but they were divorced sometime later. Paula was born in Los Angeles on June 19, 1963. Good conversation starters could be about old boyfriends, including television star John Stamos (Jesse on *Full House*) and radio personality Brian Phelps (of KLOS's morning team, Mark and Brian). If you catch her on a good day, she has no problem with pictures and autographs. However, some days she seems too busy. Rating: 6.

# Bryan Adams

Bryan Adams is a highly successful musician who has had hit songs on the charts for over ten years. He was born in Canada on November 5, 1959. Bryan dropped out of high school to concentrate on his musical career. In the 1980s he had a dozen hits. Good conversation starters would include anything Canadian, especially hockey. Additionally, he produced a band called Glass Tiger for Capitol Records that had two hit songs. Bryan has said that this was one of his top achievements. He is very down-to-earth and usually has no problem taking pictures or signing autographs. Rating: 7.

# Don Adams

Don Adams is the genius behind Maxwell Smart, Secret Agent 86 of Control in the old television series *Get Smart*. He also starred in *The Nude Bomb*, the movie version of *Get Smart*. He recently re-created his role in *Get Smart* on the Fox network. Don was born in New York City on April 13, 1926. A good conversation starter would be about his voice-over work on the children's cartoon *Inspector Gadget*. Don Adams is a great guy who can't do enough for fans or admirers. His picture accessibility is very high; he would probably even supply the film if you asked. When you run into Don, tell him hello from Bret and Steve. Rating: 10

# Andre Agassi

Andre Agassi is one of the top men's tennis players in the world. He has won Wimbledon as well as the United States Open. He is also very visible as a spokesman for the Canon Rebel camera and Nike shoes. Andre was born in Las Vegas on April 29, 1970. His father began to groom Andre as a world-champion tennis player almost from birth. As a toddler Andre hit tennis balls with Jimmy Connors, and as a teenager he was shipped off to Nick Bolletieri's Tennis Academy in Florida. He spent time in the academy with his current tennis rival, Jim Courier. A good conversation starter would be anything to do with Las Vegas. Andre is very loyal to his hometown, and, in fact, he has had two streets named after him near his house. Other topics would include his "good" friends, including Barbra

Streisand and Brooke Shields. Andre is great when it comes to meeting the public. As I pointed out earlier in the book, he bought us lunch when we met him at the airport. Rating: 9.

## Troy Aikman

Troy Aikman is the celebrity quarterback for the Dallas Cowboys. He was the youngest quarterback in history to win two Superbowls and was the MVP of the Superbowl in 1993. He received the largest rookie contract in the history of football after he was drafted number one in 1989 out of the University of California, Los Angeles (UCLA). His contract was worth over $11 million for six years. Good conversation starters would include his love of country music and Superbowl trivia. Troy has had relationships with country singer Laurie Morgan and Janine Turner of television's *Northern Exposure*. He was born in Cerritos, California, in November 1966. You could also ask him about when he was recruited by University of Oklahoma coach Barry Switzer, who is currently his head coach with the Dallas Cowboys. Troy does a lot of charity work. Off the field, he is very accessible to pictures and autographs. However, while at "work" he is all business. Rating: 7.

## Alan Alda

Alan Alda is best known as Benjamin Franklin "Hawkeye" Pierce on television's *M*A*S*H*. He has been writing, directing, and acting in movies ever since. Following *M*A*S*H*, he starred in *California Suite, Same Time Next Year, The Seduction of Joe Tynan, The Four Seasons, Sweet Liberty, A New Life, Crimes and Misdemeanors, Betsy's Wedding, Whispers in the Dark, And The Band Played On, Manhattan Murder Mystery*. Good topics of conversation with Alda are women's rights (he is a huge supporter of the Equal Rights Amendment, and women's rights in general) and his college, Fordham University. He is also very involved in theater. He received an Emmy nomination for *And The Band Played On* in 1994. He is very proud of his family, including his wife of thirty-seven years and three daughters. Alda was born in New York on January 28, 1936, and is a survivor of childhood polio. His real name is Alphonse D'Abruzzo. We have met Alan Alda twice, and he seemed cold. You need to be very careful in approaching Alda if you want to strike up a good conversation. Rating: 5.

## Jason Alexander

Jason Alexander has catapulted to stardom as George on the hit sit-com *Seinfeld*. His background is in Broadway—in fact, he won the Tony Award for best actor in 1989. Good conversation starters would include the fact that he began going bald as a teenager—he seems very proud of it. He also did a song-and-dance routine that brought down the house to open the 1993 Comedy Hall of Fame Awards. Alexander was born Jay Scott Greenspan in Newark, New Jersey, on September 23, 1959. He has been nominated for an Emmy Award for his work on *Seinfeld* and has become a cult hero. Steve and I have met him many times and he is always quite approachable. We have had many lengthy conversations with Jason. Rating: 9.

## Muhammad Ali

Muhammad Ali is the legendary boxer who was the three-time heavyweight champion of the world. He is commonly regarded as one of the top boxers of all time. He changed the sport by bringing personality to the boxing ring. Good conversation starters would include his on-again-off-again friendship with Howard Cosell and his personal friendship with Elvis Presley. Ali lives on a farm outside Kalamazoo, Michigan. He was born Cassius Clay in Louisville, Kentucky, on January 17, 1942. He changed his name to Muhammad Ali while he was heavyweight champ when he became a Black Muslim. His newly found religion forced him to refuse to go to Vietnam, on principle. Boxing stripped him of his title during the controversy over his military service. Muhammad is suffering from Parkinson's disease and is difficult to approach. Rating: 4.

## Tim Allen

Tim Allen is best known as Tim the Tool Man on the hit television show *Home Improvement*. Tim is also a bestselling author, top stand-up comedian, and movie star. In 1994 *Home Improvement* maintained its status as a top-five show, his book was among the top five bestsellers for the year, and his movie, *The Santa Clause*, was a blockbuster. Tim was in advertising before he was arrested for dealing cocaine. He spent over two years in jail. Once out, he began his show business career as a stand-up comic, quickly becoming one of the hottest comedians on the club circuit. His trademark comedy routine about male "macho" earned him a shot at a sitcom and he has made the best of it with *Home Improvement*. A good conversation starter with Tim would be his involvement in race-car driving (he participates in the Celebrity Grand Prix of Long Beach) or his early work in Mr. Goodwrench commercials. He was born in Denver on June 13, 1953, and went to college at Western Michigan University. Tim is very nice to talk to, but it always seems that no time is the right time to take a picture with him. Rating: 5.

## Woody Allen

Woody Allen is a world-famous actor, director, and writer. He won the Academy Award for directing *Annie Hall* in 1977. He also won Academy Awards for Best Screenplay for *Annie Hall* in 1977 and *Hannah and Her Sisters* in 1986. Some early movies you could bring up with Woody include *What's New Pussycat*, for which he wrote the screenplay and in which he starred; *Take the Money and Run*, in which he starred, directed, and cowrote the screenplay; *Bananas*; *Everything You Always Wanted to Know About Sex* (*But Were Afraid to Ask)*; and *Sleeper*. He is an avid musician and plays clarinet religiously. A good conversation starter would include New York sports teams, particularly basketball's Knicks. Woody was born Allen Stewart Konigsberg in Brooklyn, New York. His birthday is December 1, 1935. He has some weird habits including taking his temperature every two hours during the day. Woody is very difficult to approach. He is not very interested in conversation with the public, much less in pictures or autographs. If you do approach him, work out your plan carefully. Rating: 3.

## Kirstie Alley

Kirstie Alley is best known for her role as Rebecca on the television show *Cheers*. She also starred in the blockbuster movie *Look Whose Talking*, as well as in its sequels. She got her start playing a Vulcan in *Star Trek II: The Wrath of Khan*. Kirstie is married to actor Parker Stevenson, who starred in television's *The Hardy Boys*. She was born in Wichita, Kansas, on January 12, 1955. A good conversation starter might be her *Look Whose Talking* costar John Travolta, who is back in the limelight after his last film, *Pulp Fiction*, won so much critical praise. Another conversation starter might be her home, which was once Al Jolson's. She is a big environmentalist. Kirstie is unbelievably nice to the public. The few times we have met her, she has been nothing but gracious. She is always open for pictures and autographs. Rating: 8.

## Carol Alt

Carol Alt is one of the few models who are classified as "supermodel." She has been on more magazine covers than you can count. Carol was born in New York on December 1, 1960. Good conversation starters would include her experience as spokesmodel for CoverGirl makeup. She is fairly accessible, but always seems to be in a hurry, rushed off by "her people." Rating: 5.

## Loni Anderson

Loni Anderson originally made her mark as the bombshell receptionist Jennifer Marlowe on television's *WKRP in Cincinnati*. She has also starred in a number of television movies. Loni made headlines as the wife of Burt Reynolds, and even more headlines when they divorced. Loni's divorce from Burt was one of the favorite topics of the tabloids for quite a while. She was born on August 5, 1946, in St. Paul, Minnesota. A good conversation starter would be her stint as a detective on television alongside Lynda Carter. The two times we have met Loni Anderson, she was with Burt Reynolds, and they were both very nice. Since her divorce we haven't heard of her appearing in public very often, so her accessibility seems to have changed. However, based on the two occasions we spoke with her, Rating: 7.

## Richard Anderson

Richard Anderson is one of the best actors to ever work in television. His exposure to the general public is fairly limited, but his most famous role makes him a classic. He was Oscar Goldman on television's *The Six Million Dollar Man* and proved the strength of his role by being just as convincing as Oscar Goldman on television's *The Bionic Woman*. He was born in New Jersey on August 8, 1926. We have never had the honor of meeting Richard, but we have heard nothing but good things about him and his accessibility. Rating: 7.

## Richard Dean Anderson

If you need someone to make a bomb out of a paper clip and a stick of chewing gum, Richard Dean Anderson is your man—at least, the character he played on television is your man. Anderson played the title role in the hit television series *MacGyver*. A good conversation starter would be his hobby of driving race cars. He was born on January 23, 1950, and his hometown is Minneapolis. Richard seems to be a genuinely nice guy. He will normally take pictures and sign autographs and seems open to conversations that you might initiate. Rating: 7.

## Mario Andretti

Mario Andretti is one of the greatest race-car drivers of all time. He is a legend on the racing circuit. He has won the Indianapolis 500 and every other major Indy car-racing title. A good conversation starter could be his two sons, who are also race drivers. In fact, his son, Michael Andretti, is also a top racer. Mario Andretti was born in Italy on February 28, 1940. Rating: 6.

## Ann-Margret

Ann-Margret is probably most famous for her role as Elvis Presley's leading lady in the motion picture *Viva Las Vegas*. She has made over thirty movies during her career and has also appeared on Broadway. She was born in Sweden on April 21, 1941. Her full name is Ann-Margret Olsson. A good conversation starter would be her having served as a model for the character Ann-Margrock on the television animated sitcom *The Flintstones*. Also, many of Elvis's friends say Ann-Margret should have been the girl Elvis married. Ann-Margret is the embodiment of "old Hollywood." She is a classic "movie star." She is very good with the public and will sign autographs and take pictures. Rating: 8.

## Adam Ant

Adam Ant is most famous as the lead singer of the music group Adam and the Ants. He and his band were very popular in the very early eighties. He fired the Ants and continued to record as Adam Ant. As a solo artist he had a number of Top Forty hits, including "Puss 'n' Boots," "Goody Two Shoes," "Apollo 9," and "Friend or Foe." A good topic of conversation could be his first band deserting him to form the hit group Bow Wow Wow, or his hiring of Malcolm McLaren, the Sex Pistols manager, as a career consultant. Adam Ant's real name is Stuart Goddard and he was born in England on November 3, 1954. Since his music successes, he has been involved in acting. He starred with Pierce Brosnan in the motion picture *Nomads*. Adam Ant is very accessible. He is always willing to take pictures or sign autographs. Rating: 8.

## Michael Anthony

Michael Anthony is the bass guitar player for the rock band Van Halen. He plays a guitar that looks like a giant bottle of Jack Daniel's whiskey onstage during Van Halen's concerts. A good topic of conversation with Michael would be a very early bootleg of a Van Halen concert, taped at the Pasadena Civic Center, in which the band was introduced as "Van Halaman." Michael was born June 20, 1955, in Chicago. He is by far the most approachable member of Van Halen. Rating: 8.

## Christina Applegate

Christina Applegate broke into celebrity as Kelly Bundy on the Fox network's *Married ... With Children*, which in 1995 became the longest-running sitcom currently on the air. She has also starred in the motion picture *Don't Tell Mom, the Babysitter's Dead*. Christina has become a regular staple of the teen fan magazines. She was born in Hollywood, California, on November 25, 1972. A good conversation starter with Christina would be her appearances on Los Angeles radio station KROQ's late night advice talk show, *Love Lines*. She seems pretty standoffish, and is usually difficult to approach. Rating: 4.

## Giorgio Armani

Giorgio Armani is a world-famous fashion designer. His men's suits, conveniently called Armani suits, are regarded as the best in the world by many. His suits have been featured in hundreds of motion pictures and worn by a Who's Who of Hollywood, including Sylvester Stallone, Tom Cruise, and Don Knotts. Conversation starters would include his brief stint in medical school, and his having designed the uniforms for the Italian air force. Giorgio was born in Italy on July 11, 1934. If you speak Italian, he is very accessible. If you speak English, you'll have to try a little harder. Rating: 6.

## Tom Arnold

Tom Arnold is best known as Roseanne's former husband. He started his professional career as a meat packer for Hormel, then moved on to stand-up comedy. Arnold made his television debut on Roseanne's hit television show *Roseanne*. He has since tried two sitcoms of his own, the *Jackie Thomas Show* and *Tom*. Both were taken off the air quickly. When he separated from Roseanne, their split caused many headlines. After the split, Tom became a star in his own right with a terrific performance in Arnold Schwarzenegger's big-budget motion picture, *True Lies*. He now commands a salary of more than $1.5 million per film. Tom was born in Ottumwa, Iowa, on March 6, 1959. A good conversation topic could be his recent engagement or his interest in the Planet Hollywood restaurant chain. Tom seems very cocky, and feels he is very important. He is difficult to approach. Rating: 5.

## Rosanna Arquette

Rosanna Arquette is best known as a film actress. She starred opposite Madonna in the feature film *Desperately Seeking Susan*. She also starred in *After Hours*. A good conversation starter could be her role as a hitchhiker in Blake Edwards's *S.O.B.* Another could be the musical group Toto's hit song "Rosanna," of which she is supposedly the subject. The song was number two on the pop charts for five weeks in 1982 and went on to win the Grammy for Best Record. Rosanna was born on August 10, 1959, in New York. She has appeared in *Playboy* and was on the cover in the early nineties. Rosanna is pretty down-to-earth. You should have no trouble approaching her. Rating: 8.

# Dan Aykroyd

Dan Aykroyd is now best known as a motion picture actor. He has had major hits as the star of *The Blues Brothers* with John Belushi; *Ghostbusters*, with Bill Murray and Harold Ramis; *Coneheads*, with Jane Curtain; *Trading Places*, with Eddie Murphy; *Dragnet*, with Tom Hanks; and as a supporting actor in the Academy Award–winning *Driving Miss Daisy*. He hit the big time as a member of the most successful cast of *Saturday Night Live* (SNL) which also included John Belushi, Bill Murray, Gilda Radner, Jane Curtin, and Garret Morris. A good conversation starter for Dan would be his celebrity wife Donna Dixon, his love of the harmonica, or his 1980 Grammy for the musical album *Briefcase Full of Blues*, on which he sang with John Belushi. Dan was born in Ottawa, Canada, on July 1, 1950. He has been in a lot of hit movies and knows it. Dan seems to feel that he doesn't need the aggravation of interaction with the public. We have had a difficult time approaching him. Rating: 4.

# Scott Baio

Scott Baio is best known as Chachi on the very successful television series *Happy Days* with Ron Howard and Henry Winkler. He and his character were spun off from *Happy Days*, and the television show *Joannie Loves Chachi* was born. Baio went on to star in the motion picture *Zapped*. He worked with Willie Aames, of the television show *Eight is Enough*, on that movie. The two also starred in the sitcom *Charles in Charge*, which had a lengthy run. Scott is also on the television series *Diagnosis Murder*. Good conversation starters might be his love of drums or his relationship with Erin Moran, his costar on *Joannie Loves Chachi*. Another conversation starter could be the fact that he performed at Disneyland's Space Mountain. Scott was born on September 22, 1961, in New York. He is a very nice guy and will be more than happy to talk with you or sign autographs and take pictures. Rating: 8.

## Scott Bakula

Scott Bakula was the star of the hit television series *Quantum Leap*. He is a very talented and versatile actor, and was nominated for a Golden Globe award for his work on *Quantum Leap*, as well as for a Tony Award for his work on Broadway in *Romance/Romance*. A good conversation starter could be the commercial he shot for the *Los Angeles Times* "Calendar" section about stunts in the movies, which is played in Southern California movie theaters before the main attraction starts, or his short-lived role as an attorney in Palm Springs on a television show. Scott was born in St. Louis on October 9, 1955. When we met Scott, he seemed like a regular guy. He certainly is down-to-earth. We had a great conversation with him, and you can too. Rating: 9.

## Alec Baldwin

Alec Baldwin is a major motion picture star. He is one of the hottest actors in the business. He became a big-time player when he starred in the hit movie *Beetlejuice* with Geena Davis and Michael Keaton. He went on to star in the blockbuster *Hunt for Red October*, which was the film adaptation of the Tom Clancy novel. Alec turned down the chance to revive his character in *Patriot Games*, the sequel to *Hunt for Red October*, and was replaced by Harrison Ford. Good conversation starters for Alec would include: his marriage to film star Kim Basinger; his early job as a waiter at famed nightclub Studio 54; his television debut on the soap opera *Doctors*; or his short-lived interest in law school. Alec also was a lifeguard. He was born in Massapequa, New York, on April 3, 1958, and graduated from New York University. Alec would be a great politician and is as outgoing and polite as can be to the public. Rating: 7.

## Stephen Baldwin

Stephen Baldwin is the brother of Alec. While not quite as famous, Stephen is making his own mark in the world of celebrity. He began as a Calvin Klein model and then went on to play Buffalo Bill on the television series *The Young Riders*. He has also starred in motion pictures. A good conversation starter with Stephen could be his job in a pizza place before he went into acting. Other topics could include his wife Kennya, and child, Alaia. Stephen, like his brother Alec, was born in Massapequa. He was born on May 12, 1966. Stephen is very approachable and is happy to sign autographs and take pictures. Rating: 7.

## William Baldwin

William Baldwin, as you might have guessed, is another brother in the famous Baldwin clan. While not as famous as Alec, he has appeared in many motion pictures. He was in Oliver Stone's blockbuster and Academy Award winner *Born on the Fourth of July*, starring Tom Cruise, and he was a star of the blockbuster Ron Howard film, *Backdraft*, which also starred Kurt Russell and Robert De Niro. William was born in Massapequa in 1963. Like his brothers, William is very accessible. Rating: 7.

## Bob Barker

Bob Barker is one of the great game-show hosts. As host of *The Price is Right*, Bob has logged more hours of original television-time than almost anyone else. Bob made headlines recently when he was sued by a former model on *The Price is Right* for sexual discrimination. A good conversation starter with Bob would be anything about animal rights, as Bob is a big supporter of animals. In fact, Bob ends each *The Price is Right* episode by asking viewers to have their pets spayed and neutered. Bob was born in Darrington, Washington, on December 12, 1923. When it comes to getting autographs and pictures, Bob is pretty much in the middle of the pack. He will sign or pose sometimes, and other times, he just won't. Rating: 5.

## Ellen Barkin

Ellen Barkin is known for her starring roles in motion pictures. In her most famous role, she starred opposite Al Pacino in *Sea of Love*. She was in the hit *Diner*, the Academy Award–winning *Tender Mer-*

*cies*, as well as *The Big Easy*, and *Switch*. A good conversation starter with Ellen could be her home in Ireland; her husband, actor Gabriel Byrne; or her two children. Ellen was born on April 16, 1954, in New York. She studied acting for years before she ever went to an audition and worked as a waitress before she hit it big. Ellen is a little difficult to approach, so a good conversation starter is essential. Rating: 5.

## Charles Barkley

Charles Barkley is known as the "bad boy" of professional basketball. While not quite as outrageous as Dennis Rodman, Charles holds the record for the highest amount of fines during a single season—over $35,000. He is the shortest player ever to lead the NBA in rebounding—six-foot-six. He has twice been sued by fans after attacking them in the stands. A good conversation starter with "Sir" Charles could be his college, Auburn, or his rumored relationship with Madonna (Just make sure you tell him you thought the rumors were ridiculous!). Charles was born in Athens, Georgia, on December 8, 1953. While Charles does seem to have a "bad boy" image, he is approachable if you use the right technique. Be nice, and be careful not to antagonize. In fact, Charles once turned down a contract worth nearly a half million dollars to appear at trading-card shows, because he feels that the fans should never be charged for autographs. Rating: 6.

## Drew Barrymore

Drew Barrymore gained national attention as the cute kid, Gertie, in one of the biggest blockbusters of all time, *E.T.: The Extra-Terrestrial*. She comes from a long line of Hollywood stars, including Lionel and John Barrymore. Drew was featured in a Gainesburger dog food commercial at age eleven months, and made her feature-film debut at age five in *Altered States*. William Hurt also made his film debut in *Altered States*, and John Larroquette (*Night Court* and *The John Larroquette Show*) played an X-ray technician in that film. At age seven, Drew became a sensation in *E.T.* At age fourteen she wrote *Little Girl Lost*, her autobiography, which chronicled her bout with alcohol and drugs. Drew says that David Crosby of the musical group Crosby, Stills and Nash helped her overcome her addictions. She became a model for Guess after Claudia Schiffer left the post. Drew starred in the hit movie *Bad Girls* in 1994 with Andy MacDowell, and also played Amy Fisher in *The Amy Fisher Story*. A good conversation starter with Drew would be her short-lived television series *2000 Malibu Road*. She appeared nude in the January 1995 edition of *Playboy*. Drew's real name is Andrew Barrymore. Unless you're hanging out in a club where Drew happens to be, you will have a tough time approaching her. Rating: 4.

## Mikhail Baryshnikov

Mikhail Baryshnikov is a world-renowned ballet artist. He has also starred in motion pictures, most notably *White Nights* with Gregory Hines, for which he won critical acclaim for his strong on-screen presence, both as dancer and actor. He currently tours with his ballet company. Mikhail was born in the U.S.S.R. on January 27, 1948. He is not seen in public too often, which makes him difficult to meet. Rating: 5.

## Kim Basinger

Kim Basinger is a major motion picture star. She has starred in *The Natural* with Robert Redford, *9 1/2 Weeks* with Mickey Rourke, and *Batman* with Michael Keaton. She is one of the highest-paid female actors in the business today, and is married to one of the highest-paid male actors, Alec Baldwin. She was romantically linked to the musician formerly known as Prince, before she began dating Alec. Early in her career Kim guest-starred on an episode of *Charlie's Angels* and appeared in a nude pictorial in *Playboy*. Some good conversation starters could be her college life at Southern Methodist University; her early career as a model with the Ford Modeling Agency; or Braselton, Georgia, the town she purchased in 1989. She recently made headlines by being sued for pulling out of the movie *Boxing Helena*. She lost the suit and was forced to file for bankruptcy. She was born in Athens, Georgia, on December 8, 1953. Kim is very nice in person and was very cordial all three times Steve and I met her. Rating: 8.

## Warren Beatty

Warren Beatty is one of the top actors working in motion pictures. His skill is critically acclaimed, and he is a huge box office attraction. His films have won over forty Academy Award nominations. Warren was nominated for an Oscar for his work in his first movie, *Splendor in the Grass*, in which he starred opposite Natalie Wood. He starred in *Bonnie and Clyde*, which won ten Oscar nominations. He won the Academy Award for best director for his film *Reds*. He has also starred in the hits *Shampoo*, *Heaven Can Wait*, *Dick Tracy*, and *Bugsy*. Warren was also involved in one of the biggest flops in Hollywood history, *Ishtar*, in which he starred with Dustin Hoffman. Good conversation starters with Warren would be his sister, Shirley MacLaine, or his original job as a bricklayer. Warren was born on March 30, 1937, in Richmond, Virginia. His full name is Henry Warren Beatty. He is married to actress Annette Bening. Warren almost never gives interviews and has the reputation of being rather withdrawn. However, when Steve and I met him, he was very gracious. Rating: 7.

## Boris Becker

Boris Becker is one of the top tennis players on the professional circuit, and is considered a national treasure in Germany. Boris is a colorful character on the court and quickly became a huge fan favorite after winning Wimbledon at a very young age. He was born in Germany on November 22, 1967. A good conversation starter could be his previous position as the touring professional at the Hyatt Grand Champions Hotel in Indian Wells, California, just outside of Palm Springs. He is very cordial and is happy to sign autographs and take pictures. Rating: 8.

## Jim Belushi

Jim Belushi is famous for his work in motion pictures and for being the younger brother of the late John Belushi. Jim began his career in show business in the shadow of his older brother, but has since created his own place as a star. He had some good supporting roles early on, including one in *The Man With One Red Shoe* with Tom

Hanks and another in *About Last Night* with Rob Lowe. He had his first hit starring with Arnold Schwarzenegger in *Red Heat* and followed that up with the hit *K-9*. Other movies have included *Who's Harry Crumb?* with John Candy, *Curly Sue,* and *Diary of a Hitman*. Jim was born in Chicago on June 15, 1954. A good conversation starter would be his extensive work with charity. Jim is very likable and is happy to talk to the public. He will have no problem signing autographs or taking pictures. Rating: 8.

## Johnny Bench

Johnny Bench is a Hall of Fame baseball player. He is commonly regarded as one of the best catchers ever to play the game. He played for the Cincinnati Reds. After he left baseball, he continued to be in the spotlight with his television commercials for a paint company, in which he would always say, "No runs, no drips, no errors." A good conversation starter with Johnny would be his love of golf—he is quite good. In addition, he loves baseball, and a good baseball question will usually spark his interest. When Steve and I met Johnny we discussed former baseball players and their chances of being elected to the Hall of Fame. Johnny is more than willing to sign an autograph for you, as long as it is for you. If he thinks you are asking for autographs to sell, he will refuse. He has no problem with pictures. Rating: 7.

## Tony Bennett

Tony Bennett is a world-famous singer. He is most widely remembered for the song "I Left My Heart in San Francisco," for which he won Grammy Awards in 1962. He has seen a resurgence in his popularity over the past few years, sparked by his son managing his career. He has been adopted by the MTV generation and was nominated in 1995 for a Grammy Award for his *MTV Unplugged* album. A good conversation starter with Tony would be the fact that he began using the name Tony Bennett after Bob Hope introduced him that way during a performance in 1950. Tony's name at birth was Anthony Dominick Bennedetto, and he used the name Joe Bari for a while. He was born in Astoria, New York, on August 3, 1926. Steve and I have met Tony many, many times and he has been nothing but nice. He can't do enough for friends, fans, and the public. He is a genuinely nice man. Rating: 9.

## Candice Bergen

Candice Bergen is the star of the hit television show *Murphy Brown*. She is the daughter of Edgar Bergen, who was famous as a ventriloquist. Candice says that she grew up being second best to her father's ventriloquist prop, Charlie McCarthy, and that the dummy had a bigger bedroom than she did and even had more clothes. Additionally, there are very few pictures of Candice as a small child that don't include the dummy. It seems she had a very untraditional rivalry within her home; she felt that she had to compete against the dummy. Candice attended the University of Pennsylvania, but flunked out after two years. She then signed up with the Ford Modeling Agency and did quite well. She also tried her hand at becoming a photojournalist and her work was published in *Playboy* and *Life* magazines. She covered the 1976 Democratic Convention. She then decided her life was going nowhere and reevaluated her priorities, writing her autobiography, *Knock Wood*, which discussed her rivalry with her father's dummy. In 1987, she worked hard to win the role of Murphy Brown and was cast. She has gone on to win the Emmy Award for Best Actress in a Comedy Series for her work on *Murphy Brown*. A good conversation starter with Candice would be successful long-distance relationships, as she and her husband, film director Louis Malle, live apart (she in California, he in Europe). Candice was born in Beverly Hills, California, on May 9, 1946. The three times Steve and I have met Candice, she was a little full of herself. If you are going to approach her for conversation, pictures, or autographs, be careful. Rating: 3.

## Corbin Bernsen

Corbin Bernsen made his mark in entertainment as the womanizing divorce lawyer Arnie Becker on the hit television series *L.A. Law*. He also starred in the hit movie *Major League* with Charlie Sheen and Tom Berringer. Corbin was born in Los Angeles on September 7, 1954. A good conversation starter with Corbin would be his appearance on the 1992 Emmy Awards. Corbin is always willing to talk with the public. He is very funny, and Steve and I have had numerous conversations with him. He is very willing to take pictures and sign autographs. Rating: 8.

## Larry Bird

Larry Bird is the legendary basketball player who almost single-handedly turned around the Boston Celtics when he joined the club. He played basketball at the college level for Indiana State and joined the Celtics for the 1979–80 season. He was a great three-point and free-throw shooter, and is generally regarded as having one of the best outside shots of all time. He was born in West Baden, Indiana, on December 7, 1956. He led the Boston Celtics to three world championships during his tenure with the team. A good conversation starter with Larry might be the way he joined the Celtics. The Celtics GM, Red Auerbach, who has a history of unbelievable deals, drafted Larry for the team in 1978, after Bird had made it clear that he would be continuing in college and playing for Indiana State his senior year. After that announcement, no team wanted to waste their draft pick on Bird. Auerbach drafted Bird anyway, with the sixth pick overall. League rules stated that no professional team could talk with a college player. So, Auerbach just sat back and waited for Larry to play the next year at Indiana State. When the school year ended, Auerbach had about two weeks left to sign Bird before he was eligible to go into the draft again. Auerbach signed him, pulling off one of the greatest moves in basketball history. The loophole Auerbach used to draft Bird has since been closed. Larry is very down-to-earth. He still lives in Indiana and is as nice to the public as he could be. When you meet Larry, you will have no problem starting a conversation or getting him to sign autographs and take pictures. Rating: 8.

## Clint Black

Clint Black is a famous country music singer. His first album, *Killin' Time*, was released in 1989 and was an instant success. The title single raced up the charts and reached number one. He has enjoyed success ever since. Clint is married to actress Lisa Hartman. A good conversation starter with him would be his brief appearance in the film *Maverick*, starring Mel Gibson, Jodie Foster, and James Garner. Clint was born in Long Branch, New Jersey, on February 4, 1962. As with most country artists, Clint is very outgoing and nice to the public. He will stand around all day signing autographs and taking pictures with fans. Rating: 8.

## Robert Blake

Robert Blake is most famous for his title role in the hit television drama *Baretta*. A good conversation starter with Robert might be the cockatoo he carried around on his shoulder on *Baretta*. Robert's real name is Michael Gubitosi. He was born on September 18, 1933, in Nutley, New Jersey. Robert is a little difficult to talk to. However, with a good opening line he will open up. Rating: 5.

## Steven Bochco

Steven Bochco is one of the most successful television producers of all time. His current hit on television is *NYPD Blue*. Other television shows he has created and produced are the hits *L.A. Law* and *Hill Street Blues*. He was offered the presidency of CBS Entertainment in 1987. Good conversation starters would be his father's talent at the violin, or his own early work as a scriptwriter on *Ironside*. He created one of the weirdest television shows in recent history, the musical-cop-show-drama *Cop Rock*, which had stories similar to *Hill Street Blues*, but with the characters (policemen, criminals, attorneys, etc.) all breaking into song. It was a strange experiment that failed rather quickly. It debuted in September 1990 and was off the air before the beginning of the new year. Bochco has won many Emmy awards, including the award for Outstanding Drama Series for *Hill Street Blues* in 1981, 1982, 1983, and 1984; and the award for Outstanding Drama Series for *L.A. Law* in 1987 and 1989. Steven was born in New York City on December 16, 1943. He is a great guy and very approachable. Steve and I talked about television development with him at the 1994 Golden Globe Awards and he was very informative. He is happy to sign autographs and take pictures. Rating: 8.

# Michael Bolton

Michael Bolton is a world-famous singer, who has been very successful singing pop tunes throughout the late eighties and early nineties. He won a Grammy Award for Best Pop Vocal in 1989 for his song "How Am I Supposed to Live Without You." And repeated that feat in 1991, for his performance on the song "When a Man Loves A Woman." He also won two American Music Awards in 1992. A good conversation starter for Michael would be his appearances as the warm-up act for the hard-rocker Ozzy Osbourne in the eighties. Also, you could talk with him about songs he wrote early in his career for Cher and Barbra Streisand. Michael's real name is Michael Bolotin. He was born in New Haven, Conneticut, on February 26, 1953. How receptive Michael will be when you approach him depends on his mood at the time. Steve and I have met him when he was very gracious and fun to talk to, but we have also met him when he had a distinctly negative attitude. Rating: 4.

# Danny Bonaduce

Danny Bonaduce is most famous as the red-headed ten-year-old con man, Danny, on The *Partridge Family*. Danny went on to cope with the pressures of being a famous child actor. He has been in the news for his brushes with the law, including an incident in which he allegedly got into an altercation with a cross-dressing prostitute. Danny is currently the host of a top-rated radio talk show in Chicago. Good conversation starters with Danny would include the fact that The *Partridge Family* was loosely based on the real-life musical group the Cowsills. Danny was born on August 13, 1959. He seems genuinely happy to be back in the limelight and is happy to talk with the public. When you approach him he will be happy to sign autographs and take pictures. Rating: 7.

# Jon Bon Jovi

Jon Bon Jovi is most famous for being the lead singer of the rock band Bon Jovi. Jon's cousin, Tony Bongiovi, owned New York's world-famous recording studio the Record Plant, and Jon began his career working there. He would go get lunch for the artists and em-

Steve with U2 lead singer Bono

ployees, clean up, and do just about any odd job asked of him. He approached Polygram records about a record deal and they were impressed. They signed him to a deal but forced him to accept a few career decisions. First, he had to change his name to Jon Bon Jovi from his birth name of John Bongiovi. Second, they would only sign *him* to a deal, not his band. He had to talk his band into becoming his employees. The band Bon Jovi released its debut album in 1984 and enjoyed a great deal of success. Jon Bon Jovi released a solo album in 1990 entitled *Blaze of Glory*. Good conversation starters with Jon would include his brief appearance in the feature film *Young Guns II* or his on-again, off-again friendship with radio megastar Howard Stern. Jon was born in New Jersey on May 2, 1962. He is a little cold when approached. Steve and I have talked with him a few times, and have gotten pictures with him. However, he doesn't seem to have a good time at public events, at least not at the events where we have seen him. Rating: 5.

## Bono

Bono is the lead singer of one of the most successful bands of all time, U2. U2's albums have been at the top of the charts since their first one in 1979. Bono is one of the most prolific and successful songwriters in modern music. His real name is Paul Hewson. He began singing at an early age in his home country of Ireland. Friends began to call him Bono Vox, which loosely translated means good voice. As time went on, his nickname was shortened to Bono. When he began recording with U2, their music was labeled Christian Rock because of its lyrics. U2 slowly moved away from that type of song and lyric, but maintained its incredible popularity. Bono's world travels while on tour with U2 changed his view of religion. He became disillusioned with religion because of the suffering of children and poverty he saw around the world. U2's releases have always reflected Bono's political and social views. U2 is currently one of the top three most successful bands currently active (the Rolling Stones and Guns 'N' Roses being the other two). U2 sells out stadiums all over the world. Bono was born in Dublin, Ireland, on May 10, 1960. A good conversation starter with Bono would be the band the Dalton Brothers, which was actually the members of U2. The Dalton Brothers opened for U2 during a stadium concert in Southern California in 1987. Bono has won many Grammy Awards, including Album of the Year, for *Joshua Tree* in 1987; Best Video, for "Where the Streets Have No Name" in 1988; Best Rock Performance, for "Desire" in 1988 and for *Achtung Baby* in 1992. Steve and I met Bono at the 1994 Grammy Awards at Radio City Music Hall in New York City. He created quite a stir, and seemed to make a huge impression on the crowd. Even with such notables as the members of Aerosmith, business giant Donald Trump, singing legend Frank Sinatra, and the top music-makers of the year attending the event, Bono seemed to have the most impact on the hall. Still, when Steve and I approached him, he was terrific. He offered us one of his smokes—either a small cigar or brown-wrapped cigarette, we're not sure. He was very gracious. We took pictures with him and had a great conversation. Rating: 9.

## Sonny Bono

Sonny Bono gained entry into the limelight as half of the very popular duo Sonny and Cher. Sonny and his wife, Cher, worked in clubs around the country before they landed their own television series, the *Sonny and Cher Comedy Hour*, in 1971. The show became a huge hit, and Sonny became a huge celebrity. In 1974, Sonny and Cher divorced. The two each tried their hand at separate television shows. Sonny started the *Sonny Comedy Revue* on ABC in the fall of 1974. The show failed, as did Cher's attempt. The two reunited professionally in 1976 for the television show the *Sonny and Cher Show*. That show lasted two years. Sonny went on to guest-star on a number of television shows, including *Blossom*, the *Love Boat*, *Love American Style*, and *Hotel*. Sonny has since gone on to politics. He ran for and won election as the mayor of Palm Springs, California. In 1994, he ran for and won a seat in the United States House of Representatives. Sonny Bono was born Salvatore Bono in Detroit on February 16, 1935. Being a politician, he is very approachable if you can get to him. He is always smiling and happy to talk to you, sign autographs, and take pictures. He will probably even kiss your baby if you ask. Rating: 7.

## David Bowie

David Bowie is one of the most accomplished musical artists of our time. His songs and albums have become classics in popular music. Some of his most famous albums are *Ziggy Stardust and the Spiders From Mars* and *Let's Dance*. David is known as the Thin White Duke. He has been featured in a number of motion pictures, including *The Man Who Fell to Earth* in 1976, the critically acclaimed *Merry Christmas, Mr. Lawrence* in 1983, *Into the Night* with Jeff Goldblum and Michelle Pfeiffer, and *The Hunger* with Catherine Deneuve. He also played Pontius Pilate in *The Last Temptation of Christ*. A good conversation starter with David would be his work in the band Tin Machine. David was born in England on January 8, 1947. His real name is David Jones. He is married to supermodel Iman. David is very difficult to talk to. He will sign autographs if you push a pen and paper toward him, but he will very rarely pose for a picture. Rating: 3.

## Marlon Brando

Marlon Brando is commonly regarded as one of the greatest American actors of all time. He started out doing theater and made a name for himself there. In 1947, he played Stanley Kowalski on stage in *A Streetcar Named Desire*. In 1950, Brando made his first film, *The Men*. In 1951, he re-created his role as Stanley Kowalski in the feature-film version of *A Streetcar Named Desire*. He was nominated for an Academy Award for Best Actor for this performance. In 1952, he was again nominated for the Best Actor Oscar, for *Viva Zapata!* He was nominated for Best Actor a third time for his role as Mark Antony in *Julius Caesar* in 1953. In 1954, he had an even more spectacular year. Not only did he star in the classic *The Wild One*, but he was again nominated for the Best Actor Oscar for his role in *On the Waterfront*. This nomination was different, however, in that he won the award. Over the next eighteen years, Brando slowly ran his career into the ground. With disappointment after disappointment, he was considered something of a has-been. In 1972, he had to audition for the role of Don Corleone in the film *The Godfather*. He won the part and went on to win another Best Actor Oscar for his performance. He followed *The Godfather* with the controversial *Last Tango in Paris*, which received an X rating, but for which he was again nominated for an Oscar. Since then, his work has covered the spectrum. He was in *Apocalypse Now* as well as *Superman*. He was in *The Dry White Season* (for which he was again nominated for an Oscar) as well as in *The Freshman*. He seems to pick his roles based on his need for money. Marlon Brando was born in Omaha, Nebraska, on April 3, 1924. While it is almost impossible to find the reclusive Brando, it is even tougher to talk with him. If you do get a chance, a good topic of conversation would be his love of drums, or his home—actually, his private island—in Tahiti. Brando does sign autographs occasionally, but rarely takes pictures. Rating: 3.

## Jeff Bridges

Jeff Bridges is famous as a film actor. He has starred in the hit movies, *Against All Odds*, *Tucker*, *Blown Away*, and *Jagged Edge*. He has been nominated twice for an Academy Award: first for his role in *The Last Picture Show* in 1971, and again, for his work on *Starman* in 1984. A good conversation starter with Jeff would be his ranch in Montana, or his hobbies, which include surfing and painting. Additionally, Jeff is a songwriter. He has written two songs that were purchased by Quincy Jones. When he was sixteen, he wrote a song for the movie *John and Mary* which starred Dustin Hoffman and Mia Farrow. Jeff was born in Los Angeles on December 4, 1949. He is very approachable, happy to take pictures and sign autographs. Steve

Bret with supermodel Christie Brinkley

and I have met Jeff a couple of times, the most memorable being at a party at the Atlas Bar and Grill in Los Angeles. We had a great conversation with him and his dad, Lloyd Bridges. Rating: 8.

## *Christie Brinkley*

Christie Brinkley is one of the most famous models ever. She followed very soon after Cheryl Tiegs invented the category of supermodel. Christie made a name for herself as the covergirl for the *Sports Illustrated* "Swimsuit Edition." She quickly became one of the world's most popular and recognizable models. She married singer Billy Joel and they had one child, Alexa. Christie divorced Billy Joel in 1994, and that same year was also involved in a helicopter crash while on a ski trip. A good conversation starter with Christie could be her artistic skill—she painted the picture on the cover of Billy Joel's album *River of Dreams*. Christie has appeared in an episode of *Mad About You*, and also appeared in *National Lampoon's Vacation* with Chevy Chase. Christie was born in Malibu, California, on February 2, 1954. She is a lot of fun to talk to. She is very interesting and is more than happy to talk. Christie has no problem taking pictures or signing autographs. Rating: 9.

# Matthew Broderick

Matthew Broderick is a famous stage and screen star. He created a name for himself as the computer nerd in *War Games* in 1983 and followed that up in 1985 with *Ladyhawke*, with Rutger Hauer. In 1986, he starred in his most famous role, as the title character in *Ferris Bueller's Day Off*. He has starred in a number of films since then, including *The Freshman* with Marlon Brando. Matthew won a Tony Award for his stage work in *Brighton Beach Memoirs* and won a Tony in 1995 for his first musical *How to Succeed in Business Without Really Trying*. A good conversation starter with Matthew would be his relationship with Sarah Jessica Parker, or his home, New York City. He was born in New York on March 21, 1962, and is very much associated with the city. When Steve and I met Matthew he didn't have much of a sense of humor. He might have been having a bad night, but based on his also turning down requests from other people for autographs and pictures, his rating is low. Rating: 4.

# Tom Brokaw

Tom Brokaw is the anchor of the *NBC Nightly News*. Tom began his career in journalism as a teenager, working as an announcer. After he graduated from college he took a job as a news reporter at a station in Omaha, Nebraska. He then moved to Atlanta, where he worked as a news anchor. In time he was hired by KNBC in Los Angeles, where he worked for seven years before taking a pay cut to cover Washington politics for NBC. In 1976 he became the host of the *Today* show, and in 1982 he became the anchor of the *NBC Nightly News*. A good conversation starter with Tom would be his love of jazz, or his hobbies, which include tennis and skiing. Tom was born in Webster, South Dakota, on February 6, 1940. He is very gracious and fun to meet. He has so many interesting anecdotes about stories he has covered that conversation with him is very entertaining. Rating: 9.

# Charles Bronson

Charles Bronson is best known for his starring role in the four *Death Wish* feature movies. His first movie was *You're in the Army*

*Now* with Gary Cooper. In the 1960s, he became a huge star in such films such as *The Magnificent Seven*; *The Dirty Dozen*; and *Kid Galahad*, with Elvis Presley. Charles Bronson was born Charles Buchinsky and used that name for his first seventeen films. A good conversation starter with Charles would be his early television appearance on the *Pepsi Playhouse* in the mid-1950s. Another topic could be his role as Mike Kovac on the ABC television drama series *Man With a Camera*, in which he starred for the two years it was on the air, 1958 to 1960. Charles was married to actress Jill Ireland for twenty-one years before her death in 1990. He was born in Ehrenfeld, Pennsylvania, on November 3, 1920. Bronson is a very quiet man, but is happy to take pictures and sign autographs. Rating: 7.

## Garth Brooks

Garth Brooks is one of the most influential artists in country music. He was the first country musician to "crossover" to pop music without changing his style. His album *Ropin' the Wind* was the first country album ever to reach number one on the *Billboard* pop chart. He paved the way for country music to become more popular than anyone ever imagined. His follow-up album, *The Chase*, also reached number one. At the end of 1994, his collection of greatest hits was also resting comfortably at the top of the popular music chart. He has had some of the most successful network television specials in history. Good conversation starters with Garth would include his half-time show at the Superbowl, or his early job as a bouncer at a night club. In fact, he met his wife, Sandy, at the club, when he threw her out for fighting. He has won the Grammy Award for Best Country Vocal for his song "Ropin' the Wind." He did a guest appearance on television's *Empty Nest*. Garth was born Troyal Brooks in Tulsa, Oklahoma, on February 7, 1962. He's as down-to-earth and genuine as a person could be. Garth will stand and sign autographs for hours, until every last person has gotten one. He will take pictures, or stand around and talk for as long as you will listen. Steve and I once asked him to call our friend, Barbara Michaels, to wish her a happy birthday, and he was more than happy to oblige, even using his manager's portable cellular phone. Rating: 9.

## Mel Brooks

Mel Brooks is probably best known as the man who brought us the movie *Blazing Saddles*. But much more important than that, Mel Brooks was the creator of the television masterpiece *Get Smart*, which he created with Buck Henry in 1965. In 1968, Mel wrote and directed his first movie, *The Producers*, which won him an Academy Award for Best Original Screenplay. Mel has also produced and directed a number of well-known films, including *Young Frankenstein*, *Silent Movie*, and *Robin Hood: Men in Tights*. A good conversation starter with Mel would be his service to his country during World Ward II, when he fought in the Battle of the Bulge. You could also talk about one of his first jobs, as a writer for Sid Caesar on Sid's show, *Broadway Review*. Brooks was born in New York on June 28, 1926. His real name is Melvin Kaminsky. Mel is fairly approachable. He is usually open to conversation, autographs, and pictures. Rating: 6.

## Pierce Brosnan

Pierce Brosnan is best known as the star of the hit television series *Remington Steele*. Although he had starred in movies before he started on *Remington Steele*, it wasn't until that series began in 1982 that he gained much attention. *Remington Steele* was on the air until 1987. Pierce was selected to replace Roger Moore in the James Bond film series, but the producers of *Remington Steele* would not let him out of his contract, even though the show was scheduled to go off the air. Pierce starred in a few other projects, including the film *Nomads* with Adam Ant. In 1994, it was announced that Brosnan would replace Timothy Dalton as James Bond in the next Bond movie. A good conversation starter with Pierce would be the fact that he was featured in the same *Globe* magazine issue that Steve and I were in (November 15, 1994). Another topic could be his early job with the circus. Pierce was born in Ireland on May 16, 1952. He is always happy to talk with the public and will take pictures and sign autographs. Rating: 8.

Bret with supermodel Bobbi Brown

## Bobbi Brown

Bobbi Brown is the fastest-rising star in the modeling world. She gained national attention when she won the spokesmodel competition on Ed McMahon's *Star Search* for a record number of weeks. She has since been skyrocketing to national stardom. She married rock musician Janie Lane of the band Warrant. She was the primary reason that Warrant's MTV video, "Cherry Pie", became one of the most requested videos of 1990 and the success of the video instantly took Warrant from warm-up act to headliner. Bobbi is considered bigger than Claudia Schiffer or Cindy Crawford in some parts of Europe. A good conversation starter with Bobbi would be her charity work, which includes T. J. Martell Foundation events. Bobbi is great with the public and is more than happy to sign autographs and take pictures. Rating: 9.

## Carol Burnett

Carol Burnett is most famous as the star of the *Carol Burnett Show*, which ran from 1967 through 1978 on the CBS network. In 1979, ABC carried the program. Carol then renamed the show *Carol and*

*Company*, and it ran on NBC from 1990 through 1991. Carol is also famous for tugging her ear. She is a big fan of the soap opera *All My Children*. A good topic of conversation with Carol would be her long-time friendship with Jim "Gomer Pyle" Nabors. She considers Nabors to be her good-luck charm. Carol was born on April 26, 1933, in San Antonio, Texas. She was inducted into the Comedy Hall of Fame in 1993. Carol is a little difficult to approach. You need to catch her at the right time. Rating: 4.

## George Burns

George Burns is one of the most famous of the old-time comics. He began in show business very early in life, but didn't really go anywhere until he teamed up with his future wife, Gracie Allen. The two began to gain a reputation as a very funny vaudeville team. In 1932, they appeared in the movie *The Big Broadcast*, and went on to appear in a dozen other films. In 1950 they started the *George Burns and Gracie Allen Show*, which aired live from New York every other Thursday night. In 1952, the series became a weekly show, taped for broadcast on the West Coast. In 1958, Gracie retired. George went on to do another series, *Wendy and Me*. In 1975, George made a comeback to the world of movies with *The Sunshine Boys*, for which he won an Oscar for Best Supporting Actor. He has since gone on to star in a number of movies, including the very successful *Oh, God!* and its sequels. A good conversation starter with George would be his work with his son Ronnie on the television series the *George Burns Show* in 1958. You could also bring up his relationship with entertainment giant Don Knotts, who appeared on Burns's series *George Burns Comedy Week*, in 1985. At this writing George is ninety-nine-years old and is still making appearances. There isn't a nicer man in show business. George is a great guy and will be more than happy to take pictures with you. Because of his advanced age, you might want to skip the autograph. Rating: 10.

## George Bush

George Bush was the forty-first president of the United States. He served as president from 1989, when he took over from Ronald Reagan, until 1993. Before he took office as president, he served as vice president under Reagan from 1981 through 1989. Bush is a decorated veteran of World War II. He was also the director of the CIA. He currently resides in Texas. A good conversation starter with Mr. Bush would be his son's ownership of a major league baseball team. Mr. Bush was born in Massachusetts on June 12, 1924. Being a former president, Mr. Bush is protected by the Secret Service, so it is very difficult to approach him. If you do meet him at a political event or fund-raiser, he is always willing to sign autographs and take pictures. He is a very likable man. Rating: 8.

## Brett Butler

Brett Butler is the star of the hit television show *Grace Under Fire*. She started out in show business as a stand-up comedienne. A good conversation starter with Brett would be her cool first name, even if she does have an extra *t* (I spell my name *Bret*). Other topics would be her appearance on Dolly Parton's music-variety television show, *Dolly*, in 1988. Brett was born in Montgomery, Alabama, on January 30, 1958. When Steve and I met Brett at the 1994 Golden Globe Awards, she seemed to tolerate the public. She would take pictures and sign autographs, but she didn't seem too happy about it. Rating: 5.

## Nicolas Cage

Nicolas Cage is famous as an offbeat motion picture star. His roles usually border on the bizarre. He played a baby thief in the hit *Raising Arizona*, and a half-crazed man who loses his fiancée in a poker game in *Honeymoon in Vegas*. Other hit movies he has been in include *Moonstruck*, with Cher; *Amos and Andrew*; *Peggy Sue Got Married*, with Kathleen Turner; and the classic *Fast Times at Ridgemont High*, with Phoebe Cates. Nicolas's real name is Nicolas Coppola. He changed his name to avoid the perception that he was receiving favorable treatment in the entertainment industry because of his very famous uncle, Francis Ford Coppola. A good topic of conversation with Nicolas would be the taste of cockroaches—he ate a live one on-camera in the movie *Vampire's Kiss*. Nicolas was born in Long Beach, California, on January 7, 1964. He has another famous relative—his aunt, Talia Shire (yo, Adrianne of Rocky fans).

Nicolas is a very funny guy and is happy to meet the public. He will sign autographs and take pictures. Rating: 7.

## Dean Cain

Dean Cain is best known for playing Superman in the television series *Lois & Clark: The New Adventures of Superman*. Dean attended Princeton University with Phill Swagel and Brooke Shields. He was a very talented football player and rejected over a dozen scholarship offers. After graduation from college, Dean was drafted by the Buffalo Bills, but, due to a knee injury, never started a game. Instead he concentrated on acting, and in 1990 landed a role on the *ABC Saturday Mystery*. In 1992, he won a role on Aaron Spelling's hit television show *Beverly Hills 90210*, as Shannen Doherty's love interest. Dean was born in Mt. Clemens, Michigan, on July 31, 1966. He is very open to talking with the public and is happy to sign autographs or take pictures. Rating: 8.

## Michael Caine

Michael Caine is an accomplished motion picture actor. He may be best known for his role in *Hannah and Her Sisters*, for which he won the Oscar for Best Supporting Actor, but he also won Oscar nominations for his roles in *Alfie* (1966), *Educating Rita* (1983), and *Sleuth* (1972). However, not all his films have been critically praised. He has starred in some pretty terrible movies, like *Beyond the Poseidon Adventure*. He says that he picks roles based on the location of the shoot and the money the filmmakers are willing to pay. Some recent well-known films in which he starred include *Dirty Rotten Scoundrels* with Steve Martin, and *On Deadly Ground* with Steven Seagal. A good conversation starter with Michael could be his restaurant in London, Langan's Brasserie. Another topic could be his name, which he got from the movie *The Caine Mutiny*. His real name is Maurice Micklewhite. He was born in London on March 14, 1933. Michael is one of those celebrities who is right on the border between being nice to fans and being rude. He is tough to categorize because he can be abrasive on occasion, yet he can also be quite gracious. Rating: 5.

Steve with singer Mariah Carey

## *Mariah Carey*

Mariah Carey is a very successful singer. Her albums have topped the *Billboard* pop music charts since her debut in 1990. She was working as a waitress when she attended a party that Columbia Records president Tommy Motolla happened to be at. Mariah gave Tommy a demo tape of herself singing. After Tommy left the party, he popped the tape into his car stereo and loved what he heard. He raced back to the party, only to find that Mariah had left. Tommy found someone who had been hanging around with Mariah and got her phone number. He called her right away and left a message on her telephone answering machine. He signed her to a recording contract, and later to a marriage contract. The two were married in a ceremony that reportedly cost over a half-million dollars. Mariah is said to have viewed video copies of the Prince Charles–Lady Diana wedding for ideas for her own fairy-tale wedding. She has had a string of hit singles, including a remake of Michael Jackson's song "I'll Be There." A good conversation starter with Mariah would be her *MTV Unplugged* appearance, or her highly success-ful Christmas album, of which she is very proud. She has won sev-eral Grammy Awards, including Best Pop Vocal and Best New

Artist. Mariah was born in New York on March 27, 1970. She is very nice to the public and is always ready to take a picture or sign an autograph. Rating: 8.

## George Carlin

George Carlin made a name for himself as one of the most successful stand-up comics of all time. He has appeared on television many times, including his current show on the Fox network, the *George Carlin Show*. He also appears as a three-inch-tall character on the children's program *Shining Time Station*. George appeared as George Lester in *That Girl* with Marla Thomas. His first break came on the CBS talent variety show *The Talent Scouts* in 1962. A good conversation starter with George would be his "Seven Dirty Words," which were part of his stand-up comedy routine. Another topic would be his work on the *Tony Orlando and Dawn* variety show in 1976. George was born in New York on May 12, 1937. He has been in show business a long time and seems a little jaded. If you approach him with a subject he is interested in, you can get a conversation started. Rating: 4.

## Belinda Carlisle

Belinda Carlisle is famous for being the lead singer of the all-girl rock band the Go-Go's. She was a regular fixture in the Los Angeles punk rock scene during the late seventies. In the early eighties, the Go-Go's released their debut album, and a string of hits ensued. Some of their most famous songs include "We Got the Beat," "Our Lips are Sealed," and "Vacation." The Go-Go's broke up and Belinda embarked on an uneventful solo career. In 1994, the Go-Go's reunited for a concert tour and the release of a greatest-hits album, which did quite well. A good conversation starter with Belinda would be her relationships with Andy Taylor, guitarist for Duran Duran; and Mike Marshall, formerly of the Los Angeles Dodgers. Belinda was born in Hollywood, California, on August 16, 1958. She is very accessible and is happy to take pictures, sign autographs, or sit around and chat. Rating: 8.

## Art Carney

Art Carney was the legendary Ed Norton on *The Honeymooners* on which he starred with Jackie Gleason. *The Honeymooners* is one of the symbols of television's Golden Age. Art also starred with George Burns and Lee Strasberg in the critically acclaimed feature film *Going In Style*, which was released in 1979. In the film, Art plays a bored senior citizen who teams up with Burns and Strasberg to rob a bank in order to create some excitement in their lives. Art starred as Chief Paul Lanagan in a television series in the late 1970s *Lanigan's Rabbi*, which was rotated with *Columbo*, *McCloud*, and *McMillian* as the *NBC Sunday Mystery Movie*. A good conversation starter with Art is anything about the early days of television. Art was a pioneer, and will long be remembered for his comic style. He was born on November 4, 1918, in Mt. Vernon, New York. Art is seldom seen in public these days, but if you are lucky enough to meet him, he is a true gentleman. He will be happy to do all he can for you. Rating: 9.

## Jim Carrey

Jim Carrey is best known for his title role in *Ace Ventura: Pet Detective*. He began in show business as a stand-up comedian. His act was very bizarre. He would dislocate his shoulder and swing his arm into unnatural positions. He would kick his feet up from under himself and land flat on his back, etc. He continued his crazy stunts as a standout in the Fox television show *In Living Color*. As a member of the ensemble cast of *In Living Color*, Jim created some very memorable characters, including Fire Marshall Bill. His debut as a feature-film star was the low-budget *Ace Ventura: Pet Detective*. *Ace* turned out to be one of the biggest box office smashes of 1994 and propelled Carrey into megastar status. His second effort, *The Mask*, also turned out to be a blockbuster. Carrey followed *The Mask* with *Dumb and Dumber* in 1994. Again, Carrey had a huge hit on his hands. Roughly a hundred films in the history of movies have grossed $100 million at the box office, and Jim Carrey was the star of three of them in a row. He is also playing the Riddler in the latest *Batman* film. A good conversation starter with Jim would be his relationship with television's *Picket Fences* star Lauren Holly. Another topic would be his many nights performing at the Los Angeles comedy club, the Comedy Store. Jim was born in Canada on January 17, 1962. He is a very funny man both in the movies and in person. He is a lot of fun to meet and is happy to take pictures and sign autographs. Rating: 9.

# Johnny Carson

Johnny Carson is well known as the King of Late Night. He ruled the late-night airwaves for nearly thirty-five years. Johnny began in television as the star of *Carson's Cellar* in 1951. In 1953 *Carson's Cellar* was cancelled, and Johnny went to work for Red Skelton as a writer for the *Red Skelton Show*. When Skelton fell and received a concussion, Johnny was asked to fill in. He was such a hit that CBS gave him his own show, the *Johnny Carson Show*, which failed in less than a year. In 1957, Johnny became the host of a game show, *Who Do You Trust?* It was a big hit and led to Johnny's being asked to take over the reigns of the *Tonight* show from Jack Paar. Johnny hosted the *Tonight* show for the next three decades, until he retired in 1992. A good conversation starter with Johnny is anything about tennis, as he is a huge fan. He purchased tennis great John McEnroe's home, and, as part of the deal, demanded free tennis lessons from McEnroe. John agreed and the sale went through. Johnny was born in Iowa in October 1925. He is a great guy and is happy to meet the public. He will take pictures and sign autographs. Rating: 7.

# Jimmy Carter

Jimmy Carter was the thirty-ninth president of the United States. He has had a political rebirth in the early 1990s by using his expert negotiation skills to help ease conflicts all over the world. Mr. Carter served as president from 1977 through 1981, losing a reelection bid to Ronald Reagan. As a former president, Mr. Carter is protected by the Secret Service and is therefore very difficult to meet. Rating: 5.

# David Caruso

David Caruso became a big star as the lead in the television show *NYPD Blue*. He made a lot of headlines when he left the show in a dispute with the producers over money. David was in some very successful films before *NYPD Blue* made him famous. In 1982, he appeared in both the Oscar-winning *An Officer and a Gentleman* and the blockbuster *First Blood*, in which Sylvester Stallone introduced us to Rambo. Caruso then played Mitch, a deputy to Brian Dennehy's sheriff, in *First Blood*. He disappeared for the next decade, until his smash return in *NYPD Blue*. David was born in New York on January 17, 1956. He is rather quiet in person, but he will take pictures and sign autographs. Rating: 7.

## Dana Carvey

Dana Carvey became famous as one of the more talented members of the *Saturday Night Live* ensemble cast. He then became a star in the box office blockbuster *Wayne's World*. Dana also starred in the 1990 film *Opportunity Knocks*, with Robert Loggia. A good conversation starter with Dana would be his impersonation of George Bush. Dana was born in Missoula, Montana, on April 2, 1955. He began in show business as a stand-up comedian. Dana is very nice and always seems to be up for a conversation. I have never seen him turn down anyone for a picture or autograph. Rating: 8.

## David Cassidy

David Cassidy became famous as Keith Partridge on the *Partridge Family*. Since then he has been in a number of movies, including *Instant Carma*, and a television series, *David Cassidy: Man Undercover*, a short-lived police drama. As lead singer of the Partridge Family musical group, David sold four million copies of the song "I Think I Love You." David is the brother of Shaun Cassidy, who also had a hit song, "Da Doo Run Run." David is currently starring in theater productions. A good conversation starter would be the cartoon take-off of the Partridge Family, called *The Partridge Family 2200 A.D.* You could also ask him whatever happened to the Partridge Family tour bus. David is also related to Oscar winner Shirley Jones—she is his stepmom. David was born in New York on April 12, 1950. He is very accommodating to his fans, yet he can reach a point where he has had enough. Rating: 6.

# Phoebe Cates

Phoebe Cates became an overnight sensation after the release of the movie *Fast Times at Ridgemont High*, in which she starred as Linda. Her costars in that film included Judge Reinhold and Sean Penn, and the film also marked the film debuts of Eric Stoltz and Nicolas Cage. Phoebe followed up her *Fast Times* success with the film *Paradise*, which was similar in story line to Brooke Shields's *Blue Lagoon*, only much better. She later starred in the hit film *Gremlins* and its sequel, *Gremlins 2: The New Batch*. She has also starred in the films *Private School*, *Drop Dead Fred*, *Shag*, and *Bodies, Rest & Motion*. She is a terrific actress who has been steadily more impressive throughout her career. Phoebe is married to actor Kevin Kline. A good conversation starter with Phoebe would be her career as a teen model, or her cameo in the 1990 film *I Love You to Death*, in which she played a one-night stand of the star of the film, Kevin Kline. Phoebe is one of the most accessible celebrities we have met. She is fun, interesting, and very gracious. She is always ready to sign autographs and take pictures. Rating: 10.

# Chevy Chase

Chevy Chase gained national fame in 1975 as a cast member of the television show *Saturday Night Live* during its inaugural season. He was originally hired by Lorne Michaels, the producer of *SNL*, as a writer, but he ended up on-camera. He was the first of a very talented cast to really gain fame from *SNL*. He left the show in 1976 to pursue a movie career. After a slow start, Chase starred in *Foul Play* with Goldie Hawn, which became a hit. He followed up the success of *Foul Play* with the blockbuster *Caddyshack*, which became an instant classic due in part to a terrific performance by Bill Murray as the deranged groundskeeper. Chase went on to star in a number of flops before he starred in another winner. His next successful project was *National Lampoon's Vacation*. *Vacation* and its sequels, *European Vacation* and *Christmas Vacation*, really showcased Chase as a terrific talent. He has also starred in *The Three Amigos* with Steve Martin and Martin Short, as well as in *The Invisible Man* with Darryl Hannah. In 1993 Chase started a disastrous talk show on the Fox network. A good conversation starter with Chevy would be his love of tennis, or the way he got his first big break: He landed the job on *SNL* after meeting producer Lorne Michaels in a line at a movie theater. Chevy was born in New York on October 8, 1943. His real name is Cornelius Chase. Both times Steve and I have met Chevy he has been in a rather foul mood. He is difficult to approach. Rating: 3.

# Cher

Cher initially made a name for herself as a singer and half of the very successful *Sonny and Cher Comedy Hour*, which ran from August 1971 through May 1974, when Cher divorced her husband, Sonny Bono. In 1975 Cher tried her hand at her own television show, *Cher*. It lasted a little less than a year. In early 1976 she reunited, professionally, with Sonny and the *Sonny and Cher Show* returned, but the magic was gone and the show ended for good in 1977. Cher then went into movies. Her first few attempts were not very memorable. In 1983, however, she was nominated for an Oscar for her performance in *Silkwood*, with Meryl Streep. Her next film, *Mask*, won her the Best Actress award at the Cannes Film Festival. In 1987, she won an Academy Award for Best Actress for her work in *Moonstruck*. She has since starred in a number of films, including *The Witches of Eastwick* with Jack Nicholson; and *Mermaids* with Winona Ryder. A good conversation starter would be her elopement to Tijuana, Mexico, with Sonny, or her current hit infomercials. Cher was born Cherilyn Sarkisian La Piere in El Centro, California, on May 20, 1946. She is fairly open to autographs and pictures at big public events. Rating: 5.

# Connie Chung

Connie Chung has become one of the most famous newscasters of the 1990s. Until recently she was the coanchor for the *CBS Evening News*. She began in journalism covering George McGovern's run for the presidency in 1972, and then covering Watergate. She was teamed with Dan Rather as anchor of the *CBS Evening News* in the early 1990s. Connie was born in Washington, D.C. on August 20, 1946, two years after her father moved the family there from China. A good conversation starter with Connie would be her husband, talk-show host Maury Povich, or the Emmy Award she won for her interview with Marlon Brando in 1989. Connie is very enjoyable to meet. She is happy to sign autographs and take pictures. Rating: 8.

## Tom Clancy

Tom Clancy is one of the most successful authors in recent times. His bestselling books have been made into blockbuster motion pictures. His first effort, *Hunt For Red October*, became a bestseller and went on to gross $120 million dollars as a major motion picture starring Alec Baldwin. The sequel to *Red October* was *Patriot Games*; the book was again a bestseller, and the film adaptation, this time starring Harrison Ford, was another huge success. Next came *Clear and Present Danger*, which was the bestselling fiction book for the entire decade of the eighties, and again was a huge smash at the box office. Tom also wrote the bestsellers *Red Storm Rising*, *The Cardinal of the Kremlin*, and *The Sum of All Fears*. A good conversation starter with Tom would be the fact that Steve and I appeared as extras in his film *Clear and Present Danger*. (We used the methods in this book to get invited onto the set, and then were used as extras!) You could also talk baseball with him, since he is a part-owner of the Baltimore Orioles. Tom was born in Baltimore, Maryland. You can meet him when he does book signings, and he is usually very gracious. Rating: 7.

## Eric Clapton

Eric Clapton is a famous musician. His song "Layla" is considered a rock anthem. He was the lead guitarist for the Rock-and-Roll-Hall-of-Fame band, the Yardbirds. He was then the guitarist for the band Cream, which also is a member of the Rock and Roll Hall of Fame. He later had hits as guitarist for Derek and the Dominos, including "Layla," and has had considerable success as a solo artist, earning Grammy Awards for Record of the Year, Song of the Year, Best Pop Vocal, and Best Rock Vocal. Eric was born in England on March 30, 1945. His real name is Eric Clapp. Good conversation starters would be his friendship with Peter Townsend, of the rock band The Who. Eric seems to be very pleased with himself and does not bother to stop and talk with the public. The few times Steve and I have met

Eric, he has given very little indication that he would be willing to take pictures, sign autographs, or talk to the public. Rating: 2.

## Dick Clark

Dick Clark is most famous for his role as the host of the television show *American Bandstand*. Dick hosted *American Bandstand* in primetime for three months in 1957, and then the show was moved to daytime. It ran daily until 1963, when it became a weekly show. *American Bandstand* stayed on the air until 1987, when it was finally cancelled. Dick then began producing the show himself and sold it in syndication for another year. He has also been the host of the television game shows *The $25,000 Pyramid*, *The $100,000 Pyramid*, and *The Challengers*. A good conversation starter with Dick is his production company, Dick Clark Productions, which puts on many of the big awards shows seen on television every year, including the Golden Globes and the American Music Awards. Dick was born Richard Wagstaff Clark on November 30, 1929, in Mount Vernon, New York. He is a very nice guy, but during his productions he is all business. If you catch him when he is not working, he is happy to sign autographs and take pictures. However, when he is working he does not want to be bothered. Rating: 5.

## Andrew "Dice" Clay

Andrew "Dice" Clay is a very successful stand-up comedian. His first big break came on the *Rodney Dangerfield Young Comedian Special*. His trademark dirty nursery rhymes and tough-guy image propelled him to the top of his field. He was soon selling out fifteen thousand-seat arenas, including Madison Square Garden. Then he was hit with a social backlash critical of his jokes, which were perceived to be degrading to women and minorities. His first starring role in a motion picture occurred at the height of this backlash. We thought the film, *The Adventures of Ford Fairlane* was terrific and that it would have been a huge hit if the film company hadn't cancelled all advertising and quietly pulled the movie from theaters. While Dice has enjoyed a continuing successful career in stand-up comedy, his film potential has yet to be realized. A good conversation starter with Dice would be his self-proclaimed "second home," the Comedy Store comedy club in Hollywood. Clay is a terrific guy and always has time for the public and his fans. He will sign autographs and take pictures. Rating: 9.

## Bill Clinton

Bill Clinton is the forty-second president of the United States. He took office in 1993 after defeating George Bush in the election. He was born in Hope, Arkansas, on August 9, 1946. Mr. Clinton is constantly surrounded by Secret Service, so it is difficult to approach him. However, if you do meet him, he is a politician, and so is happy to talk with his constituents. Rating: 5.

## Glenn Close

Glenn Close is a well-known movie actress. She began her show business career on the stage, earning a Tony Award nomination for her role in *Barnum*. She then landed her first film role, as Robin Williams's mother in *The World According to Garp*, for which she received an Academy Award nomination. Her next film was equally successful for her. It was *The Big Chill*, for which she won another Oscar nomination. She went back to the stage to star in Andrew Lloyd Webber's play, *Sunset Boulevard*, for which she won a Tony in 1995. A good conversation starter with Glenn could be her childhood home, a five hundred-acre estate in Connecticut. She was born in Greenwich, Connecticut, on March 19, 1947. When Steve and I met Glenn at the Los Angeles premiere of *Sunset Boulevard*, she acted very much like a prima donna. Good luck approaching her. Rating: 2.

## Sean Connery

Sean Connery is best known as James Bond, secret agent 007. Although he had appeared in over ten movies before starring as Bond in *Dr. No*, that movie propelled him to stardom. He reprised his role as Bond in several later films, including *From Russia With Love*, *Goldfinger*, *You Only Live Twice*, and *Diamonds are Forever*. Since leaving this role, he has appeared in many films including *The Untouchables*, with Kevin Costner, for which he won an Oscar for Best

Supporting Actor; *Indiana Jones and the Last Crusade* with Harrison Ford; and *The Hunt for Red October* with Alec Baldwin. A good conversation starter would be his guest-hosting for Sammy Davis, Jr., on *The Sammy Davis, Jr., Show* in 1966. Sean was born Thomas Connery in Scotland on August 25, 1930. He is happy to sign autographs and take pictures. Rating: 7.

## Jimmy Connors

Jimmy Connors is one of the greatest tennis players ever to play the game. He won every major title in tennis, including Wimbledon and the U.S. Open. A good conversation starter with Jimmy would be his wife Patti, who was a *Playboy* Playmate, or his appearance on the television show *Saturday Night Live With Howard Cosell* in 1975. Jimmy was born James Scott Connors in Belleville, Illinois, on September 2, 1952. Jimmy is a lot of fun to meet if you're into tennis. Not only is he a legend, but he has a lot of interesting stories. He will sign autographs and take pictures. Rating: 8.

## David Copperfield

While David Copperfield is probably best known as the most famous magician since Houdini, a close second would be his status as the fiancé of supermodel Claudia Schiffer. David started learning magic as a way to impress girls, and as his engagement to Claudia can attest, it certainly paid off for him. David Copperfield gained huge popularity following his network television specials, in which he has made the Statue of Liberty disappear, walked through the Great Wall of China, and escaped from a safe locked in the basement of a building about to be blown up. David was born in New Jersey on September 16, 1956. He is a legend in Europe. Copperfield performs over three hundred shows a year, and after most shows goes out to the lobby to meet his fans, where he signs autographs and takes pictures for hours. Rating: 8.

## Francis Ford Coppola

Francis Ford Coppola is one of the most famous filmmakers of all time. He began in 1963, directing a few films that were basically flops. In 1970, he won an Oscar for his screenplay for *Patton*, and in 1972, he directed one of his finest films, *The Godfather*, for which he won Oscars for Best Director and Best Screenplay. In 1974, he made two movies, *The Godfather, Part II* and *The Conversation*. Both were nominated for Oscars for Best Screenplay and Best Picture, and *The Godfather, Part II* won both awards. His next film was the classic *Apocalypse Now*, in 1979. While it won him another Oscar nomination for Best Picture, it didn't do well at the box office. A good conversation starter with Coppola would be his home in the Napa Valley wine country of California. He is the brother of Talia Shire and the uncle of Nicolas Cage. Coppola was born in Detroit on April 7, 1939. It is rare to find Coppola out in public; however, when you do, he is usually willing to sign autographs and take pictures. Rating: 5.

## Kevin Costner

Kevin Costner is one of the biggest names in motion pictures. His most famous work is *Dances With Wolves*, for which he won multiple Academy Awards, including Best Director and Best Picture. His first big break came when he was cast as the suicide in *The Big Chill* in 1983, but his work ended up on the cutting-room floor. In 1987, he hit the big time as Elliot Ness in *The Untouchables*. In 1988 he starred in the hit *Bull Durham*, and in 1989 he starred in the classic *Field of Dreams*. Since his blockbuster success with *Dances With Wolves*, Costner has starred in Oliver Stone's *JFK*, *The Bodyguard*, and *Wyatt Earp*. A good conversation starter with Kevin could be his small part in the 1982 movie *Night Shift*, which made Michael Keaton a star and was the first big success for Ron Howard as a director. Another topic would be Kevin's college, Cal State, Fullerton. Kevin was born in Lynwood, California, on January 18, 1955. He is fairly accessible and will take pictures, sign autographs, or sit around and talk if you catch him at the right time. Rating: 6.

## Katie Couric

Katie Couric is the star of the *Today* show. She has had a remarkable career in television which began with her being banned from the CNN airwaves after she did an on-camera report the network's president didn't like. She went on to excel and is currently one of

Bret with megamodel Cindy Crawford

America's favorite hosts. Katie was born in Arlington, Virginia, on January 7, 1957. She is terrific in person and is always happy to talk with the public. She is very gracious when it comes to signing autographs and taking pictures. Rating: 8.

## Cindy Crawford

Cindy Crawford is one of the most successful models of all time. She followed Christie Brinkley to the title of THE supermodel. She launched MTV's highly successful television show, *House of Style* and has also starred in two wildly popular exercise videos. A good conversation starter with Cindy would be her spokesmodel position for Pepsi, or her marriage to actor Richard Gere. Cindy was born in De Kalb, Illinois, on February 20, 1966. She is great to meet, because not only is she very open to talking to the public, but pictures with her always come out great. Rating: 9.

## Michael Crichton

Michael Crichton will probably always be remembered as the author of *Jurassic Park*. His novel was a bestseller, but more important, the

Steven Spielberg film adaptation of it went on to gross over $300 million, making it one of the top money-makers of all time. Crichton is no stranger to the bestseller lists. He has had hits with *The Andromeda Strain*, *Westworld*, *The Great Train Robbery*, and more recently, with *Rising Sun*. His 1994 book *Disclosure* went on to become a major motion picture starring Michael Douglas and Demi Moore. A good conversation starter with Crichton would be his college, Harvard, or the fact that he had an article published in the *New York Times* when he was only fourteen years old. Michael was born in Chicago on October 28, 1942. *Michael* is his middle name; his first name is John. Crichton is very accessible at book signings. Rating: 7.

## Walter Cronkite

Walter Cronkite is still probably the most recognizable name in news. He was the anchor of the *CBS Evening News* for nearly twenty years, from 1962 through 1981. Before his reign as CBS's anchor, Cronkite was a journalist for the *Houston Post* and a correspondent for United Press International. A good conversation starter with Walter would be the image of modern news programs. He is very concerned that news programs are losing credibility. In fact, Cronkite is commonly regarded as the most trustworthy newsman ever. Another interesting fact is that during World War II, Cronkite parachuted into the Netherlands with the 101st Airborne to cover the Normandy invasion for UPI. Cronkite was born in St. Joseph, Missouri, and was raised in Kansas City, Missouri. He was born on November 4, 1916. Meeting Walter Cronkite is one of the most interesting things I've ever been a part of. He is so full of insight and information that any conversation is fascinating. Cronkite is happy to take pictures and sign autographs. Rating: 8.

## Tom Cruise

Tom Cruise is one of the most popular actors working today. His first film, *Endless Love*, was released in 1981. He was in three more films, *Taps*, *Losin' It*, and *The Outsiders*, before he really made a name for himself in the blockbuster *Risky Business* in 1983. His fame was solidified with the 1986 release of *Top Gun*. Since then, he has starred in the Academy Award–winning *The Color of Money* with

Paul Newman, in the Academy Award–winning *Rain Man*, in the Academy Award–winning *Born on the Fourth of July*, and in the blockbuster *A Few Good Men*. A good conversation starter with Tom would be the Church of Scientology, of which he is a member, or his bout with dyslexia. Tom was born Thomas Cruise Mapother IV on July 3, 1962, in Syracuse, New York. He is very polite and willing to talk with the public or take pictures and sign autographs. Rating: 8.

## Billy Crystal

Billy Crystal became famous as a gay character on the television series *Soap*. He started out in show business as a stand-up comic. After *Soap*, Billy was added to the cast of *Saturday Night Live*, where his impersonations and characters became big hits. His most notable skits on SNL had the country mimicking, "You look maaahvelous." He has gone on to star in some highly successful movies, including *When Harry Met Sally*" with Meg Ryan, and *City Slickers*. He has also starred in some bombs, including *Mr. Saturday Night* and the sequel to *City Slickers*. A good conversation starter with Billy could be his small role on *All in the Family*, or his studies at New York University. Billy was born in New York on March 14, 1947. He is very unapproachable. Steve and I have seen him be rude to almost everyone who tries to talk to him. At the People's Choice Awards (ironic because the awards are voted on by the fans), he was obnoxiously rude to a small girl who couldn't have been older than ten. She merely asked for a picture and he shot off some flippant remark. He got a good laugh out of it with his friends as he walked away from the youngster, who began to cry. Rating: 1.

## Macaulay Culkin

Macaulay Culkin reached the pinnacle of popularity when he starred in the blockbuster *Home Alone*, which made over $140 million. The sequel, *Home Alone 2: Lost in New York*, also grossed over $100 million. His first big break came when he appeared in *Uncle Buck* with John Candy. His performance was unforgettable. He has gone on to star in a half-dozen other pictures. A good conversation starter with Macaulay would be his friendship with pop megastar Michael Jackson—Culkin appeared in Jackson's video "Black or White"—or his $5-a-day allowance. Macaulay was born in New York on August 26, 1980. He is a great kid and is usually happy to take pictures and sign autographs, especially for other kids. Rating: 7.

## Jamie Lee Curtis

Jamie Lee Curtis is best known as Hannah Miller on the TV show *Anything But Love* with Richard Lewis. She went on to star in movies, most notably the 1994 blockbuster *True Lies* with Arnold Schwarzenegger. A good conversation starter with Jamie would be her role as Lt. Barbara Duran in the first season of the short-lived television show *Operation Petticoat*. Jamie was born in Los Angeles on November 22, 1958 and her father is actor Tony Curtis. She is very gracious in person. At an event in 1994, Steve and I saw her stand posed for what seemed like an eternity for a camera that just wouldn't work. She wanted to make sure that the fan got the picture. Rating: 8.

## Willem Dafoe

Willem Dafoe has become a very bankable movie star. He initially made an impact in 1985, starring in *To Live and Die in L.A.* In 1986, he won an Oscar nomination for his role in Oliver Stone's *Platoon*. He has since been in over a dozen movies, including the controversial *Body of Evidence*, with Madonna; and the blockbuster *Clear and Present Danger*, with Harrison Ford. A good conversation starter with Willem would be his first film role, in one of the biggest bombs of all time, *Heaven's Gate*. Willem was born in Appleton, Wisconsin, on July 22, 1955. He is very approachable. Steve and I spoke with him for quite a while on the movie set of *Clear and Present Danger*. He is always ready to sign autographs and take pictures. Rating: 9.

## Ted Danson

Ted Danson became a star as Sam Malone on the long-running television show *Cheers*. Ted has also starred in a number of films, the most successful being *Three Men and a Baby*, with Steve Guttenberg and Tom Selleck. Ted created quite a controversy when he was involved with Whoopi Goldberg by doing a comedy routine while in blackface at a Friar's Club function. A good conversation starter with Ted would be the sitcom pilot he did for NBC before *Cheers*, called *Dear Teacher*. Ted was born Edward Danson in San Diego, California, on December 29, 1947. The few times Steve and I have met Ted he has been very nice. He is usually open to pictures and autographs. Rating: 7.

## Geena Davis

Geena Davis is a very successful movie actress. She made her debut in 1982 in the hit *Tootsie*. In 1988 she had two huge successes: *Beetlejuice*, with Alec Baldwin and Michael Keaton, which was a box office hit; and *The Accidental Tourist*, which earned her an Academy Award for Best Supporting Actress. In 1991 she was again nominated for an Oscar, this time for Best Actress in the film *Thelma and Louise*. A good conversation starter with Geena would be her lead role in the little-known sitcom *Sara*, or her marriage to action-movie director Renny Harlin (*Cliffhanger*). Geena was born Virginia Davis in Wareham, Massachusetts, on January 21, 1957. She is very gracious and usually will sign autographs, take pictures, and talk with the public. Rating: 7.

## Jim Davis

Jim Davis is the celebrated cartoonist who created *Garfield*, which is seen in newspapers across the country, and has been turned into a children's cartoon that airs on Saturday mornings. A good conversation starter with Jim would be the process of choosing a voice for Garfield when the comic strip was developed into a television cartoon. Jim was born in Marion, Indiana, on July 28, 1945. He attends conventions and signs autographs and takes pictures. Rating: 7.

## Calvert Deforest

Calvert Deforest is the world-famous actor who brought us Larry "Bud" Melman on *Late Night With David Letterman*. He has created some unbelievable moments on the show, including the skits "Ask

Mr. Melman" and the renamed version, "due to a freak accident," "Ask Mr. Melman's Head." He has gone on to star in the exercise video *The Coach Potato Workout* and in television commercials for 1–800–COLLECT. A good conversation starter with Calvert would be two memorable skits on the Letterman show, "Melman Bus Lines" and "Toast on a Stick." Calvert was born in Brooklyn, New York, in 1923. He is very happy to take pictures and sign autographs and is a genuinely nice guy. Rating: 8.

## Rebecca De Mornay

Rebecca De Mornay is best known for playing the maniacal nanny in the 1992 blockbuster movie *The Hand That Rocks the Cradle*. She made her first big splash in *Risky Business* with Tom Cruise. Rebecca has also starred with Don Johnson in *Guilty as Sin*, and in Neil Simon's film *The Slugger's Wife*. A good conversation starter with Rebecca would be her shared birthday with Richard Gere and Michael Jackson. Rebecca was born in Santa Rosa, California, on August 29, 1962. Her father is television talk-show host Wally George. She is fairly accessible and usually will take pictures and sign autographs. Rating: 6.

## Robert De Niro

Robert De Niro is one of the most respected actors of all time. He has won two Academy Awards, the first for his supporting role in *The Godfather, Part II* and the second for Best Actor for his work in *Raging Bull*. His other landmark movies include *Taxi Driver* and *A Bronx Tale*, his directorial debut. A good conversation starter with De Niro would be Rubicon, the restaurant in San Francisco that he owns with Francis Ford Coppola. De Niro was born and raised in New York City. His birthday is August 17, 1943. He is rarely seen in public and usually turns down any requests for media interviews. He is difficult to approach. Rating: 3.

## Bob Denver

Bob Denver is a legend in the entertainment world. While he has been on many sitcoms, including *Dusty's Trail* and *The Good Guys*,

Bret with Johnny Depp

he will never be forgotten as Gilligan on television's classic hit *Gilligan's Island*. *Gilligan's Island* ran for three years between 1964 and 1967 and has been shown in reruns ever since. Three prime-time sequels were made in 1978, 1979, and 1981. Additionally, a television cartoon, *The Adventures of Gilligan* was on the air between 1974 and 1977. A good conversation starter with Bob would be the little-known fact that Gilligan had a first name, Willie. Bob Denver was born in New Rochelle, New York, on January 9, 1935 (one day after Elvis Presley). Bob is very approachable. He is happy to talk with the public, sign autographs, and take pictures. Rating: 8.

## Johnny Depp

Johnny Depp became famous as Tom Hanson on the Fox television network's hit *21 Jump Street*. He has since gained critical praise for starring roles in the feature films *Edward Scissorhands*, *Don Juan de Marco*, *What's Eating Gilbert Grape*, and the award-winning *Ed Wood*. A good conversation starter with Johnny would be his Hollywood club, the Viper Room. You could also discuss his relationship with supermodel Kate Moss. Johnny was born in Owensboro, Kentucky, on June 9, 1963. He is very gracious with the public, and more than willing to take pictures and sign autographs. Rating: 8.

## Bo Derek

Bo Derek became famous in the role of a fantasy girl in the film *10*, which starred Dudley Moore. Bo's other films include *Tarzan, the Ape Man, Bolero*, and *Ghosts Can't Do It*. Most of her films include a lot of Bo undressed. A good conversation starter with Bo could be her husband, John Derek. Bo was born in Long Beach, California, on November 20, 1956. Her real name is Mary Collins. She is hard to approach because her husband is very protective. Rating: 3.

## Danny DeVito

Danny DeVito gained national stardom as the overbearing taxi dispatcher in the hit television sitcom *Taxi*. Even before his role in *Taxi*, Danny had been in movies. He was quite good in *One Flew Over the Cuckoo's Nest* and *Goin' South*, both with Jack Nicholson. However, Danny didn't become a "movie star" until 1985 when he stole the movie *Romancing the Stone* from Michael Douglas and Kathleen Turner. He has gone on to star in two movies with Arnold Schwarzenegger, two with Michael Douglas, and one as the Penguin in *Batman Returns*. A good conversation starter with Danny would be his previous career as a hairdresser—he went by the name Mr. Danny in his sister's salon. Danny was born in Neptune, New Jersey, on November 17, 1944. He is a very dedicated artist and is very sincere in general. He is happy to talk with the public and has no problem posing for pictures and signing autographs. Rating: 8.

## Princess Diana

Princess Diana's claim to fame is the simple fact that she is the princess of Wales and is in line to become the queen. She is married to Prince Charles, but their relationship is on the rocks. Her name was Lady Diana Spencer before she married the future king of England. If you get the chance to speak with her, there are many protocols to observe. However, if given the opportunity, a good conversation starter would be her work for charity; she is tireless in this pursuit. In fact, about the only chance of meeting her is at a charity function. However, she is unbelievably gracious. Rating: 3.

## Joe DiMaggio

Joe DiMaggio carries around two distinct claims to fame. First, he is one of the greatest baseball players ever to play the game. He was a New York Yankee and is right up there with Babe Ruth and Mickey Mantle. Joe's second claim to fame is that he was married to the legendary Marilyn Monroe. A good conversation starter with Joe would be about anything baseball, or his work as "Mr. Coffee." Joe was born in Martinez, California, on November 25, 1914. While Joe is very nice to the public, he is overburdened with people trying to make money from his autograph; you will have better luck merely asking for a picture. Rating: 5.

## Shannen Doherty

Shannen Doherty became famous as Brenda on the television show *Beverly Hills 90210*. She left the show, reportedly because the producers had had enough of her attitude and antics. A good conversation starter with Shannen would be her early roles, including a starring role as Jenny Wilder on *Little House on the Prairie* from 1982 to 1983. Shannen was born in Memphis, Tennessee, on April 12, 1971. Depending on when you catch her, she can be very friendly or pretty rude. Be careful. Rating: 5.

## Phil Donahue

Phil Donahue invented one of the most successful television genres in history—the daytime talk show. He is a member of the Emmy Hall of Fame for his work on the show *Donahue*. A good conversation starter with Phil would be his guest-starring role on the television show *Blossom*, or his television show *The Last Word*, an informational news show that was on ABC in 1982 and 1983. Phil was born in Cleveland on December 21, 1935. He is married to Marlo Thomas, whom he met on his show. Phil is an exceptionally interesting man to meet. He is full of information and anecdotes, and conversations with Phil are extremely entertaining. He is always willing to sign autographs and take pictures. Rating: 9.

## Michael Douglas

Michael Douglas is a major motion picture star. His films have been top money-makers for many years. Michael's first big success was his starring role on television's *The Streets of San Francisco*, on which he worked from 1972 until 1975. He left *The Streets of San Francisco* to produce the feature film *One Flew Over the Cuckoo's Nest*. Not only was that film one of the top money-earners of the year, but it won Oscars in five categories, including Best Picture. Michael has gone on to become as famous an actor as he was a producer, with starring roles in such films as *Romancing the Stone*, *Fatal Attraction*, and *Basic Instinct*. In 1987, Michael won an Oscar for Best Actor for his role as Gordon Gekko in *Wall Street*. A good conversation starter with Michael would be his strong belief in handgun control, or the fact that he directed two episodes of *The Streets of San Francisco*. Michael was born in New Brunswick, New Jersey, on September 25, 1944. His father is acting legend Kirk Douglas. Michael is extremely open to talking with the public, signing autographs, or taking pictures. Rating: 8.

## Robert Downey Jr.

Robert Downey Jr., gained fame as one of Hollywood's Brat Pack, which consisted of a half-dozen young actors who made a big splash in films in the early eighties. Other members of the Brat Pack included Emilio Estevez, Judd Nelson, Molly Ringwald, Rob Lowe, and Demi Moore. Robert's first big success was in *Less Than Zero*. In 1992, he turned in an incredible performance as Charlie Chaplin in the film *Chaplin*, which earned him an Academy Award nomination for Best Actor. A good conversation starter with Robert would be his father, an underground filmmaker, who directed Robert in a number of his early movies. Robert was born in New York on April 4, 1965. He is very gracious and is happy to pose for pictures and sign autographs. Rating: 8.

## Clint Eastwood

Clint Eastwood gained fame as one of the best actors in the Western genre. His classics, such as *The Good, the Bad, and the Ugly*, are still very popular today—nearly thirty years after their initial release. His next huge success was as the title character in *Dirty Harry* and its sequels. In the 1990s he gained critical praise both for his acting and his directing. In 1992, Eastwood directed *Unforgiven*, which won Academy Awards in four categories, including Best Picture and Best Director. A good conversation starter with Clint would be the time he spent as mayor of his hometown, Carmel, California. Clint was born in San Francisco on May 31, 1930. He will take pictures and usually will sign autographs. It is difficult to have a conversation of any length with him unless he knows you. Rating: 5.

## Emilio Estevez

Emilio Estevez became famous as one of Hollywood's Brat Pack. Emilio's first two successes came in the Brat Pack movies *St. Elmo's Fire* and *The Breakfast Club*. Since then he has had major hits with the films *Young Guns*, in which he played Billy the Kid, and *The Mighty Ducks*. A good conversation starter with Emilio would be his famous family, which includes his father Martin Sheen, and his brother Charlie Sheen. The Sheens changed their names. Emilio was born Emilio Estevez in New York on May 12, 1962. He is pretty open to taking pictures and signing autographs, but can get a little impatient if the fans are overdoing it. Rating: 6.

## Erik Estrada

Erik Estrada will probably always be best known as Ponch on the hit television show *CHiPS* that ran from 1977 through 1983. He has since starred in some motion pictures—mostly low-budget ones. A good conversation starter with Erik would be his appearances on the television show *Whodunnit?*. *Whodunnit?* was a show that would enact a murder and then stop just before the murderer was revealed. Contestants would then match wits against an expert panel that usually included famous lawyers such as F. Lee Bailey. Erik appeared on *Whodunnit?* as an actor in the murder scenes. He was born in New York on March 16, 1949. Erik is very approachable and is happy to sign autographs and take pictures. Rating: 7.

## Fabio

Fabio became famous as a romance-novel cover model. In fact, he modeled for over 110 novel covers in one year. He has since gone on to make a bestselling calendar. A good conversation starter would be his cameo on the hit television show *Roseanne*. Fabio's full name is Fabio Lanzoni. He was born in Italy on March 15, 1961. Fabio is happy to take pictures and sign autographs. Rating: 7.

## Farrah Fawcett

Farrah Fawcett gained national attention as Jill Munroe on the hit television show *Charlie's Angels*. Although she was only on the show for one season, the show is generally remembered for her. In 1977 a poster of her was published that became the bestselling pin-up poster of all time. In 1984 she starred in the television movie *The Burning Bed*, which was one of the highest-rated television movies of all time. She has also starred in major motion pictures, including the 1986 release *Extremities*. A good conversation starter with Farrah would be *Good Sports*, the sitcom she did in 1991 with her husband Ryan O'Neill. Farrah was born February 2, 1947, in Corpus Christi, Texas. She is generally approachable and usually has no problem with pictures or autographs. Rating: 7.

## Barbara Feldon

Barbara Feldon had the privilege of playing the girlfriend and then wife, of one of the most remembered television characters of all time—Maxwell Smart, Secret Agent 86 of Control. Barbara played 99, Max's steady partner. A good conversation starter with Barbara would be her co-hosting role on the 1974 television show the *Dean Martin Comedy World*. Barbara's real name is Barbara Hall. She was born in Pittsburgh, Pennsylvania, on March 12, 1941. She is exceptionally nice and is happy to accommodate her fans. Rating: 8.

## Bridget Fonda

Bridget Fonda is best known for her role in the motion picture hit *Single White Female*. She first gained attention starring with Phoebe Cates in *Shag* and she also starred in the blockbuster *Point of No Return*. A good conversation starter with Bridget would be her family, including her aunt, Jane Fonda; her father, Peter Fonda; and her grandfather, Henry Fonda. Bridget was born in Los Angeles on January 27, 1964. She is a little tough to approach, but if you can start the conversation off well, you have a better shot. Rating: 6.

## Harrison Ford

Harrison Ford's films have grossed more than any other actor's in history. A 1994 list of the highest grossing films of all times includes these movies of Ford's: Number 3, *Star Wars*; number 5, *Return of the Jedi*; number 9, *Raiders of the Lost Ark*; number 11, *The Empire Strikes Back*; number 18, *Indiana Jones and the Last Crusade*; and number 23, *Indiana Jones and the Temple of Doom*. And, this list doesn't include the later box office smashes *Patriot Games* and *The Fugitive*. A good conversation starter with Harrison would be the title of Box Office Star of the Century, which he was given by the Theater Owners Association of America in 1994. Harrison Ford was born in Chicago on July 13, 1942. He travels with a bodyguard who tries to keep people away. However, if you do have the opportunity to talk to Ford, he is very gracious. Rating: 5.

## George Foreman

George Foreman recently became boxing's oldest heavyweight champion ever. George's battle with Muhammad Ali is legendary. This classic bout, when Ali used the "rope-a-dope" strategy to beat Foreman for the heavyweight title, is one of the great boxing matches of all time. George tried his hand at acting in the early nineties with the sitcom *George* on the Fox network. A good conversation starter with George would be the commercials he did for Doritos with his four children—all named George. Big George was born in Marshall, Texas, on January 10, 1949. He is a very entertaining guy with a great sense of humor and is usually happy to sign autographs and take pictures. Rating: 8.

## Jodie Foster

Jodie Foster first became famous at age thirteen, when she was nominated for an Academy Award for playing a prostitute in *Taxi Driver*. Years before, however, she started in show business as the little girl in the Coppertone suntan lotion television ads. Since her success with *Taxi Driver*, she has won two Academy Awards, one for *The Accused* and the other for *Silence of the Lambs*. A good conversation starter with Jodie would be her ability to read at the age of three. Her real name is Alicia Foster. She was born in Los Angeles on November 19, 1962. When Steve and I met Jodie we were surprised that she was so nice. She is happy to take pictures and sign autographs. Rating: 9.

## Michael J. Fox

Michael J. Fox became famous as Alex P. Keaton, the staunch Republican, on the hit television series *Family Ties*. He won three consecutive Emmy awards for his performances on the show. While still starring in *Family Ties*, Michael began his movie career and hit it big with the blockbuster *Back to the Future*. He later starred in that movie's two sequels. Another of his movies is one of my personal favorites: *Doc Hollywood*. A good conversation starter with Michael is anything about hockey, as he is a big fan. Another topic could be the fact that his real middle initial is *A*.—Michael's full name is Michael Andrew Fox. He was born on June 9, 1961, in Canada. He is married to Tracy Pollan, who also appeared on *Family Ties*. Michael is very nice and will take pictures and sign autographs. Rating: 7.

## Peter Gabriel

Peter Gabriel achieved stardom as one of the members of the rock band Genesis. He quit the band in 1975 to pursue a solo career. As a solo artist he has flourished, scoring with hits such as "Shock the Monkey," "Sledgehammer," and "Big Time." A good conversation starter with Peter would be his visionary music videos. He is a pioneer in the field. Additionally, you could discuss his CD-ROM computer program, which allows you to remix some of his songs and create your own versions of his videos. Peter was born in England on May 13, 1950. Steve and I met Peter hanging around the press tent at the American Music Awards. He was very interesting and had no problem posing for pictures. Rating: 8.

## Andy Garcia

Andy Garcia is famous as a star of motion pictures. He was first recognized as a "star" after the release of *The Untouchables* with Kevin Costner in 1987. Since then, he has been nominated for an Oscar for his work in *The Godfather, Part III*. A good conversation starter for Andy would be the fact that he was in the pilot for *Hill Street Blues*. Andy was born in Cuba on April 12, 1956. He is fairly approachable and usually doesn't have a problem with autographs or pictures. Rating: 5.

## James Garner

James Garner may be best known as James Rockford in the television hit *The Rockford Files*, which ran from 1974 through 1980. However, before that Garner was a star of the television hit *Maverick*. He also starred in the popular feature film *Support Your Local Gunfighter*. Recently, he starred in the movie version of *Maverick* with Mel Gibson and in the HBO original movie *Barbarians at the Gate*. A good conversation starter with James would be the Purple Heart Award he won in the Korean War, or his Oscar nomination for Best Actor for his performance in the 1985 movie *Murphy's Romance*. James was born James Baumgarner in Norman, Oklahoma, on April 7, 1928. He does take pictures and sign autographs, but sometimes it is difficult to start a conversation with him. Rating: 5.

## Richard Gere

Richard Gere gained movie star status after his role in *Looking for Mr. Goodbar* in 1977. He went on to star in a number of other hits, including the 1980 movie *American Gigolo*; the 1982 megahit and Oscar winner *An Officer and a Gentleman*; and 1992's biggest hit, *Pretty Woman*, with Julia Roberts. Gere is married to supermodel Cindy Crawford. A good conversation starter with Richard would be the fact that two of his most famous roles, in *An Officer and a Gentleman* and *American Gigolo* had been turned down by John Travolta. Richard Gere was born in Philadelphia on August 29, 1949. He is difficult to approach unless you are a student of the Dalai Lama, as is Gere. Rating: 4.

## Leeza Gibbons

Leeza Gibbons attained national stardom as the cohost of TV's *Entertainment Tonight* with John Tesh. She currently is the host of the talk show *Leeza*, which is syndicated nationally. *Leeza* is commonly regarded as one of the best shows of its kind on television, due in large part to Leeza's terrific personality and charisma. A good conversation starter with Leeza would be some of her most famous guests, including Steve and me. Another topic would be her husband, who is architect Stephen Meadows. Additionally, Leeza was the host of *George Schlatter's Funny People*. Leeza was born March 26, 1957. Her hometown is Irmo, South Carolina. She is a lot of fun to meet and is always happy to talk with the public, pose for pictures, and sign autographs. Rating: 9.

## Mel Gibson

Mel Gibson hit the big time in the low-budget film *Mad Max*, which became a box office smash in Australia. The two sequels also became huge hits worldwide. Some of Mel's other hits include *Lethal Weapon*, and its sequels; and *Maverick* with James Garner. A good conversation starter with Gibson would be the fact that he got the role in *Mad Max* because he went to the audition the day after he was in a big fight and his face looked the worse for wear. Another topic could be his having been voted the Sexiest Man in America by *People* magazine. Mel was born in Peekskill, New York, and moved to Australia as a child. He was born on January 3, 1956. Mel is fairly reserved and usually tries to avoid the public. Rating: 4.

## Kathie Lee Gifford

Kathie Lee Gifford first rose to national fame as the cohost of *Live with Regis and Kathie Lee*. She has become a national treasure. Before her stint on *Live* she was a regular on *Good Morning America*. Her autobiography, *I Can't Believe I Said That*, was a bestseller. A good conversation starter with Kathie would be her role as spokesmodel for Carnival Cruise Lines, or her singing of the National Anthem at the 1995 Superbowl. Kathie is married to football legend Frank Gifford. Her maiden name is Kathie Lee Epstein. She was born in France on August 16, 1953. She is a real pleasure to meet and always has time for her fans, happy to sign autographs and take pictures. Rating: 9.

## Paul Michael Glaser

Paul Michael Glaser became a sensation as David Starsky on the hit police drama *Starsky and Hutch*. He has gone on to direct feature films, including the 1987 hit *The Running Man* with Arnold Schwarzenegger. A good conversation starter would be the car Glaser drove in his role as Starsky—a 1974 Ford Torino painted bright red with a white stripe. Glaser was born in Cambridge, Massachusetts, on March 25, 1943. He is very gracious and has no problem with pictures or autographs. Rating: 7.

## Danny Glover

Danny Glover achieved stardom with his critically acclaimed role in *The Color Purple*. He went on to star in the blockbuster *Lethal Weapon* (and its sequels) as well as in the hit *Grand Canyon*. A good conversation starter with Danny would be his early job as a cab driver. He was born in San Francisco on July 22, 1947. Danny is very open to taking pictures and signing autographs, and you should have no problem approaching him. Rating: 8.

## John Goodman

John Goodman became famous as Dan Connor on the hit television show *Roseanne*. He starred as Babe Ruth in the 1992 hit *The Babe*,

Steve with *Cheers* and *Frasier* star Kelsey Grammer

as the king of England in *King Ralph*, and as Al Pacino's partner in the 1989 hit *Sea of Love*. A good conversation starter with Goodman would be the fact that he is the voice behind the "In 'n' Out Burger" radio commercials. John was born in St. Louis on June 20, 1952. He is great to the public and always seems to have time to talk with people, sign autographs, and take pictures. Rating: 8.

## *Kelsey Grammer*

Kelsey Grammer earned his place in the spotlight as the psychiatrist Frasier Crane on the hit television series *Cheers*. Kelsey has parlayed his *Cheers* success into another television hit, *Frasier*, a spin-off of *Cheers*. He started out in show business on the daytime soap opera *Another World*. A good conversation starter with Kelsey would be his charity work for the T. J. Martell Foundation. Grammer was born on St. Thomas in the Virgin Islands on February 20, 1955. He is exceptionally open to conversation with the public, is very down-to-earth, and has no problem signing autographs or taking pictures. Steve and I have met Kelsey a number of times, most notably right after he won an Emmy for Best Actor in a Comedy Series, when Steve and I were filming our adventures for *Dateline NBC*. Rating: 9.

## Wayne Gretzky

Wayne Gretzky is considered to be the best hockey player ever. He won the Most Valuable Player Award eight straight years (1980–1987) and has been the National Hockey League's top scorer eleven times during his incredible career. Wayne was traded to the Los Angeles Kings from the Edmonton Oilers and single-handedly raised the attendance of the Kings home games. Before Wayne came to L.A., the Kings record for sell-outs in a season was eight; in Wayne's first year, the Kings sold out thirty-nine games, and the attendance has not dropped off at all in the years since. A good conversation starter with Wayne would be golf, which is a big hobby of his. Other topics would be his wife, actress Janet Jones; his position as spokesman for the Sharp line of video cameras; or this book, Wayne loved it when we showed him an early copy. He was born in Canada on January 26, 1961. Wayne is incredibly generous with his time and has no problem talking with the public, signing autographs, and taking pictures. Rating: 9.

## Andy Griffith

After Andy Griffith brought us the *Andy Griffith Show* and introduced the world to one of the greatest actors ever, Don Knotts, his place in showbiz lore was secure. Andy went on to star in another hit television series, *Matlock*. A good conversation starter with Andy would be the spin-offs generated from the *Andy Griffith Show*, including *Gomer Pyle U.S.M.C.* and *Mayberry RFD*. Another topic would be Ron Howard, who got his start as Opie on the *Andy Griffith Show*. Andy was born in Mount Airy, North Carolina, on June 1, 1926. Andy is a true gentleman and you will have no problem approaching him. Rating: 8.

## Melanie Griffith

Melanie Griffith had been in a few films before starring in *Working Girl* in 1988. Her performance in that earned her an Academy Award nomination for Best Actress. She has gone on to star in a number of films, including *Pacific Heights*, with Michael Keaton; *Bonfire of the Vanities*, with Tom Hanks and Bruce Willis; and *Born Yesterday*, with her husband, Don Johnson. A good conversation starter with Melanie would be her early career as a teenage model. She was born in New York on August 9, 1957, but was raised in Hollywood. Melanie is fairly approachable and is usually open to signing autographs and taking pictures. Rating: 6.

## John Grisham

John Grisham is one of the top novelists working today. His best-selling novels include *The Firm*, which became a huge hit in its motion picture version starring Tom Cruise; *The Client*, which also was a box-office smash as a film starring Susan Sarandon; and *The Pelican Brief*, which starred Julia Roberts in the film version. Grisham was an attorney when he began writing novels. A good conversation starter with John would be the fact that his wife edits his books, or his love of baseball—he was a little league coach. Grisham can be found doing book signings, and so is usually easy to approach. Rating: 7.

## Charles Grodin

Charles Grodin has starred in many classic movies. He was in *The Lonely Guy* with Steve Martin, and *Midnight Run* with Robert De Niro. He also starred in the blockbuster *Beethoven* in 1992 and its sequel in 1993. Before that he was a standout in the 1978 Academy Award–winning film *Heaven Can Wait* with Warren Beatty. Charles is currently hosting a very creative and entertaining talk show on CNBC. He is an Emmy Award–winner. A good conversation starter with Charles would be his role in the 1981 movie *The Great Muppet Caper*. Charles was born in Pittsburgh, Pennsylvania, on April 21, 1935. He is very friendly and seems to genuinely love the public. His interesting personality makes him a pleasure to talk to. Rating: 9.

## Matt Groening

Matt Groening is the genius who brought the world *The Simpsons*. He started out with a successful comic strip, *Life in Hell*. A good conversation starter with Matt would be the name of his child, Homer (the same as the father character in *The Simpsons*). Another topic would be his early job at a sewage plant. Many celebrities have had guest spots on *The Simpsons*, including Ringo Starr, Tony Bennett, Danny DeVito, Johnny Carson, Luke Perry, and the rock bands Aerosmith and the Red Hot Chili Peppers. Matt was born in Portland, Oregon, on February 15, 1954, and currently resides in Venice, California. He attends comic and book conventions so he is easy to find and very accessible. He is happy to sign autographs and pose for pictures. Rating: 7.

## Gene Hackman

Gene Hackman gained stardom in 1967 when he was nominated for an Academy Award for his performance in *Bonnie and Clyde*. In 1976 he won the Academy Award for Best Actor for his work in *The French Connection*. He again won an Oscar in 1992, for Best Supporting Actor in Clint Eastwood's *Unforgiven*. Gene has appeared in dozens of films in his career. Recently he was in the blockbuster *The Firm*. A good conversation starter with Gene would be his cameo in the 1974 film *Young Frankenstein*. Hackman was born Eugene Hackman in San Bernardino, California, on January 30, 1930. He is fairly approachable and usually doesn't have a problem with signing autographs or taking pictures. Rating: 7.

## Linda Hamilton

Linda Hamilton is best known as Sarah Conner in Arnold Schwarzenegger's hit film *The Terminator*. She also starred in the hit television show *Beauty and the Beast*, which ran from 1987 through 1990. A good conversation starter with Linda would be one of her early roles in the 1982 film *Tag: The Assassination Game*. At the premiere of that film, her costar, radio legend Frazer Smith, drove an army tank down the streets of Westwood, California, for his arrival. Linda is very gracious and has no problem talking with fans or taking pictures and signing autographs. Rating: 8.

## Tom Hanks

Tom Hanks has emerged as the one of the most talented and bankable movie stars working today. He first gained fame in 1980 as Kip

Wilson on the television hit sitcom *Bosom Buddies*. Following the sitcom's cancellation, Hanks starred in the motion picture *Bachelor Party*, which became a classic film in the *Animal House* genre. In 1984 he starred in the hit *Splash* with Darryl Hannah and John Candy and in 1986 he starred with Jackie Gleason in the great film *Nothing in Common*. He was nominated for an Academy Award in 1988 for his performance in Penny Marshall's film *Big*. In 1993, Hanks took his stardom to another level. First he had the megahit *Sleepless in Seattle*, and then the critically acclaimed *Philadelphia*, for which he won the Academy Award for Best Actor. In 1994, he maintained his success with one of the biggest money-makers of all time, *Forrest Gump*, and won an Academy Award once again for his work in the title role. A good conversation starter with Tom would be his guest appearance on the television classic *Happy Days*. He was born in Concord, California, on July 9, 1956. Steve and I met Tom recently and were surprised at how approachable he is. He is currently the hottest actor working, yet he had plenty of time for people who came up to talk with him. He was happy to sign autographs and take pictures. Rating: 9.

## Daryl Hannah

Daryl Hannah made her first big "splash" (no pun intended) in the world of show business in the 1981 film *Blade Runner* with Harrison Ford. She went on to star with Tom Hanks in the blockbuster *Splash*, in which she played a mermaid. She also appeared in the Academy Award–winning film, *Wall Street* with Charlie Sheen and Michael Douglas and in the 1989 tear-jerker *Steel Magnolias*. She has been romantically linked with Jackson Browne and John F. Kennedy, Jr. A good conversation starter with Daryl might be the Andrew Lloyd Webber musical *Sunset Boulevard*; she attended the premiere in Los Angeles. Daryl is a little difficult to approach, but, if you catch her at the right time, she will take pictures. Rating: 4.

## David Hasselhoff

David Hasselhoff gained fame as the costar of a customized Trans Am named KITT, in the television series *Knight Rider*. The show was a hit from 1982 through 1986. David went on to star in *Bay-*

*watch*, which reportedly is watched by over a billion people *every day* around the globe. Hasselhoff is a legend in Europe for his music. His albums are top sellers and he plays concerts to crowds in the tens of thousands. A good conversation starter with David would be the character Kay Morgan on *Baywatch*, which is played by Pamela Bach, his real-life wife. Another topic could be his early appearances on the daytime soap opera *The Young and the Restless*. David was born in Baltimore on July 17, 1952. He is extremely approachable. Steve and I have met David a dozen times and every time he has agreed to every request made of him by the public. Rating: 9.

## Rutger Hauer

Rutger Hauer first made an impact in the United States as a terrorist in the 1981 film *Nighthawks*, starring Sylvester Stallone. Before that he had been gaining international attention in a number of films. In 1982, he was in *Blade Runner* with Harrision Ford and Daryl Hannah. He has since made a name for himself as a talented actor both in action films and traditional dramas. Most recently he was nominated for a number of awards, including a Golden Globe for his 1994 work on the HBO original movie *The Fatherland*. A good conversation starter with Rutger would be his 1987 film *Wanted: Dead or Alive*, which featured Gene Simmons of the band Kiss as the bad guy. Rutger was born in the Netherlands on January 23, 1944. He is moderately approachable and will sign the first few autographs and take the first few pictures, but he tires of attention rather quickly. Rating: 5.

## Goldie Hawn

Goldie Hawn initially became famous as one of the standouts on the television series *Laugh-In*. She has since gone on to become a major movie star, with such hit films as *Private Benjamin*, *Foul Play*, *Bird on a Wire* and *Death Becomes Her*. A good conversation starter with Goldie would be her "husband" (they're not actually married), Kurt Russell, or the movie they did together, the very funny *Overboard*. Another good topic of conversation would be her home in Pacific Palisades, California. Goldie was born on November 21, 1945 in Washington, D.C., and has never changed her name. She is very personable and usually has no problem meeting the public. Rating: 7.

# Sherman Hemsley

To describe Sherman Hemsley's fame, one only needs to use two words: George Jefferson. The television hit *The Jeffersons* was on the air for ten years, from 1975 through 1985. It was a spin-off of the hit television series *All in the Family*. George Jefferson was seen as the black counterpart to Archie Bunker. In 1986, Sherman again had a hit, this time as the star of television's *Amen*, which cast him as a deacon. *Amen* ran through 1991. A good conversation starter with Sherman would be his voice-over work as the dinosaur B. P. Richfield on the big-budget television series *Dinosaurs*. Sherman was born on February 1, 1938, in Philadelphia. He is fairly approachable and usually will sign autographs and take pictures. Rating: 6.

# Marilu Henner

Marilu Henner gained fame as Elaine Nardo on the hit television series *Taxi*, which ran from 1978 to 1983 and also launched the careers of Tony Danza, Judd Hirsch, Danny DeVito, Andy Kaufman, and Christopher Lloyd. In 1990 she again had a hit on her hands, playing Ava Evans Newton on the television sitcom *Evening Shade*. She has proved herself to be a terrific talent. In 1994 Marilu launched a refreshingly original talk show, which is gaining in popularity every day. A good conversation starter with Marilu would be her hometown of Chicago, where she was born on April 6, 1952. She always has time for the public and is very approachable and extremely gracious. Rating: 9.

# Judd Hirsch

Judd Hirsch gained fame in the hit television show *Taxi*, on which he played Alex Rieger, a cab driver who helped everyone with their problems. Judd won two Emmy Awards for Outstanding Lead Actor in a Comedy Series for his performances on *Taxi*. After *Taxi* ended its five-year run, Judd began a new series, *Dear John*, in 1988. In that, he played John Lacey, a recently divorced man who interacted with other members of his support group. The show was another huge success for Judd. A good topic to start a conversation with Judd would be the two police dramas he starred in before *Taxi*: In *Detective in the House* (1985) he played Press Wyman and in *Delvecchio* (1976–1977) he played Sgt. Dominick Delvecchio. Judd is a nice guy and is usually happy to talk with the public, sign autographs, or take pictures. Rating: 7.

## Dustin Hoffman

Dustin Hoffman is one of the most talented actors in motion pictures. His credits include some of the best films ever made. In 1967 he catapulted to stardom with his leading role in the film *The Graduate*, which earned him an Academy Award nomination. He was again nominated for an Academy Award in 1969 for his famous role as Ratso Rizzo in *Midnight Cowboy*. He has won two Oscars, for his starring roles in *Kramer vs. Kramer* in 1979 and in *Rain Man* in 1988. A good conversation starter with Hoffman would be the Emmy Award he won for his role in *Death of a Salesman*—a very rare television appearance for him. Hoffman was born in Los Angeles on August 8, 1937. Dustin is fairly approachable and usually will sign autographs and take pictures. Rating: 6.

## Bob Hope

Bob Hope is one of the most famous comedians of all time. He has had successes in almost every entertainment medium. Starting in the late 1930s, he scored with box office movie hits such as *Road to Singapore* with Bing Crosby, and its six sequels. He then scored on television, beginning with the *Chrysler Theatre* in 1963 and continuing with his yearly television specials for NBC, which show no signs of stopping. Bob is very well known for entertaining United States troops overseas. A good conversation starter with Bob would be his wife Dolores; she is about the only thing he loves more than golf. Bob was born Leslie Hope in England on May 29, 1903. He is a little difficult to approach because his handlers try to keep people a safe distance away. However, if you do get a chance to talk with him, he is very funny and happy to pose for pictures. Rating: 6.

## Anthony Hopkins

Anthony Hopkins is one of the most critically acclaimed actors currently working. He is probably best known as Hannibal Lecter in *Si-*

*lence of the Lambs*, for which he won an Academy Award for Best Actor in 1991. He is also a very accomplished stage actor. Hopkins was again nominated for an Oscar in 1993 for his performance in *The Remains of the Day*. A good conversation starter with Hopkins would be his 1993 knighting by the Queen of England, which made him "Sir" Anthony Hopkins. Hopkins was born in South Wales on December 31, 1937. He is fairly accessible, when you can find him. Steve and I met Hopkins in 1992 following his success with *Silence of the Lambs,* and he was very gracious. Rating: 7.

## Dennis Hopper

Dennis Hopper gained fame in the 1969 film *Easy Rider*, which he starred in, directed, and cowrote. He appeared in many movies over the next decade, but didn't make much of an impact. In 1979, he appeared in *Apocalypse Now*. In 1986, he regained his popularity and the industry's respect in *Blue Velvet*, a strange film by David Lynch. Since then he has played in a number of high-profile roles, including a deranged bomber in the 1994 megahit *Speed*. A good conversation starter with Dennis would be two of his early films, *Giant* and *Rebel Without a Cause*, in both of which he acted with film legend James Dean. Another topic could be the restaurant he owns in Hollywood, California, Thunder Roadhouse. Dennis was born in Dodge City, Kansas, on May 17, 1936. He is difficult to approach. However, if you use a very good opening line, he will talk to you briefly and you just might get a picture. Rating: 4.

## Whitney Houston

Whitney Houston made her mark as one of the most successful recording artists of the 1980s and 1990s. Her songs have consistently been at the top of *Billboard*'s pop charts. Two of her biggest songs have been "Saving All My Love for You" and "I Will Always Love You." In 1992 she starred with Kevin Costner in the hit feature film *The Bodyguard*. A good conversation starter with Whitney would be early television appearances on *Silver Spoons*, or her marriage to Bobby Brown. Whitney was born in Newark, New Jersey, on August 9, 1963. She is very nice if you can get to her, but she is whisked around by "her people", limiting your opportunities. Rating: 5.

Bret with *Mad About You*'s Helen Hunt

## Ron Howard

Ron Howard became a star at the age of six when he was cast as Opie on the *Andy Griffith Show*. He next had a hit with a starring role in the movie *American Graffiti*. Soon after, he became the star of one of the biggest television hits ever, *Happy Days*. He is currently one of the hottest directors in the business, with such hits as *Splash*, *Cocoon*, *Backdraft*, and *The Paper* to his credit. A good conversation starter with Ron would be the fact that he puts his brother Clint in almost every movie he directs. Ron was born in Duncan, Oklahoma, on March 1, 1954. He is fairly accessible and usually will take the time to sign autographs and take pictures. Rating: 6.

## Helen Hunt

Helen Hunt is currently the star of one of television's hottest shows, *Mad About You*, with Paul Reiser. Before her role as Jamie Buchman on *Mad About You*, Helen made a number of appearances in feature films. Some of her most notable films include *Trancers*, in 1985, and its sequel, *Trancers II*, in 1991; Billy Crystal's 1992 movie *Mr. Saturday Night*; and the 1986 hit movie *Peggy Sue Got Married*. Helen was born in Los Angeles on June 15, 1963. She is very nice in person and is always happy to take pictures or sign autographs. Rating: 8.

## Billy Idol

Billy Idol became famous as a rock musician in the eighties with such hits as "White Wedding" and "Rebel Yell." His trademark white hair and sneer are legendary in the music community. A good conversation starter with Billy would be his love of motorcycles. Another topic would be his fascination with Elvis Presley. Billy collects Elvis memorabilia and even hired one of Elvis's old bodyguards. His real name is Billy Broad. He was born in England on November 30, 1955. Billy is always willing to take pictures, sign autographs, or just sit around and talk. Rating: 9.

## Janet Jackson

Janet Jackson originally became famous as the little sister of megastar Michael Jackson. However, throughout the eighties and nineties she has been so successful at her own pop career that she has been outselling her famous older brother. She has had many hits, including "That's the Way Love Goes" and "Rhythm Nation." A good conversation starter with Janet would be her other career, as a child actor on the sitcoms *Diff'rent Strokes* and *Good Times*. Janet was born in Gary, Indiana, on May 16, 1966. She is very difficult to approach, as most of the Jacksons tend to be. However, if you do meet her, she is very nice. Rating: 5.

## Michael Jackson

Michael Jackson is perhaps the most successful singer of all time. He began as the lead singer of the very popular Jackson Five, which scored with several number one hits, including "ABC" and "I'll Be There." In the late seventies Michael released his first solo album *Off the Wall*. It sold over nine million copies and Michael was well on his way to superstardom. In 1982 he released his next album, *Thriller*, which became the bestselling record of all time, with over fifty million copies sold. He had seven top-ten hits from the album, including "Billie Jean" and "Beat It." A good conversation starter with Michael would be Quincy Jones, who was instrumental in his career. Michael was born in Gary, Indiana, on August 29, 1958. He is married to Elvis Presley's daughter, Lisa Marie Presley. Michael is guarded like Fort Knox and is almost impossible to meet. If you do get the opportunity, however, he is terrific. When Steve and I met Michael we were very surprised that all of the images we had of him—that he is extremely weird, that he talks strangely, that he wears too much makeup, etc.—were untrue. He was very "normal." His rating is low because he is difficult to meet, but if the ratings were based on a star's personality, he would rank very high. Rating: 4.

## Mick Jagger

Mick Jagger is the lead singer of one of the most successful and enduring rock bands of all time, the Rolling Stones. The Stones have had eight number one songs, including "(I Can't Get No) Satisfaction," "Get Off My Cloud," "Angie," and "Brown Sugar." A good conversation starter with Mick would be his induction into the Rock and Roll Hall of Fame. Mick also starred in the 1992 feature film *Freejack*. Mick was born in England on July 26, 1943. He is very difficult to approach and you have to be very careful about asking for pictures and autographs. Rating: 3.

## Peter Jennings

Peter Jennings is best known as the anchor of ABC's *World News Tonight*. Jennings originally held the position in 1964 when, at age twenty-six, he became the youngest network news anchor ever. He left the job after three years and went back to reporting in the field. He held the position of chief foreign correspondent for some time. In 1983, he returned to the anchor job at *World News Tonight* and has held that post ever since. A good conversation starter with Peter would be his first "anchor" position, as host of *Peter's People*, a children's show. He was nine at the time. Peter is very interesting and very gracious when you meet him. He is happy to take pictures and sign autographs. Rating: 9.

# Billy Joel

Billy Joel has been making hit music for decades. He is best known as the singer-songwriter of the classic "Piano Man," and the song title has been attached to him as a nickname. His piano-playing is legendary, and he has had more hits than one can count, including "It's Still Rock and Roll to Me," "Tell Her About It," and "Just the Way You Are." Billy Joel was married to supermodel Christie Brinkley. A good conversation starter with Joel would be his early boxing career. Billy was born in New York on May 9, 1949. He is very difficult to approach. The few times Steve and I met Billy he was in a rather foul mood. This might be because each time we met him he had just lost some award, but we can only go by our experience. Rating: 3.

# Elton John

Elton John has been on the top of the pop charts for over twenty years. In the seventies he was playing to sold-out crowds in stadiums around the world and was known for his wild costumes and wacky eyeglasses. Throughout the eighties and nineties he has toned down his wild image, but has maintained his musical success. Some of Elton's best known songs include "Crocodile Rock," "Bennie and the Jets," "Don't Let the Sun Go Down on Me," "Rocket Man," and "Philadelphia Freedom." A good conversation starter with Elton would be soccer. He is a big fan and, in fact, once owned a professional team. Elton's real name is Reginald Dwight. He was born in England on March 25, 1947. He is very difficult to approach. He doesn't like to take pictures and seems to dislike autographs as well. Rating: 3.

# Don Johnson

Don Johnson became a star playing the hip undercover detective Sonny Crocket on the hit television series *Miami Vice* from 1984 through 1989. His trendy clothes became a staple at night clubs all over the country. He has also starred in a number of feature films, including the 1990 movie *The Hot Spot*, the 1991 film *Harley Davidson and the Marlboro Man*, and the 1993 hit *Guilty as Sin*. Don was married to actress Melanie Griffith. A good conversation starter with Don would be an early television role in which he played Jefferson

Davis Prewitt on the series *From Here to Eternity* in 1980. Don is very approachable. He is happy to talk with the public and has no problem with photos or autographs. Rating: 8.

## Tommy Lee Jones

Tommy Lee Jones became a huge star following his Oscar-nominated performance in Oliver Stone's feature film *JFK*. He followed that up with the 1992 blockbuster *Under Seige* with Steven Seagal. In 1993, he won an Oscar for his performance in *The Fugitive*, with Harrison Ford. A good conversation starter with Tommy would be the fact that his roommate at Harvard was United States Vice President Al Gore. Tommy graduated from there cum laude. He was born in San Saba, Texas, on September 15, 1946. He is fairly approachable and usually has no problem with pictures or autographs. If you use a good opening line to start a conversation, Tommy is happy to sit around and talk. Rating: 7.

## Michael Jordan

Michael Jordan is arguably the greatest basketball player ever to play in the NBA. He was the NBA's leading scorer seven times, the league's most valuable player three times, and was elected to the All-Star team seven times. He retired following the 1993 season and attempted a professional baseball career as a member of the Chicago White Sox organization and played in the minor leagues. He returned to the Chicago Bulls and the NBA in 1995. A good conversation starter with Michael would be golf, at which he is excellent. Jordon was born in New York on February 17, 1963. He is a very approachable and likable celebrity. Don't ask for too many autographs, as he is certainly aware that people constantly try to make money from his signature. Rating: 7.

## Michael Keaton

Michael Keaton became a movie star with his classic performance in *Night Shift* with Henry Winkler in 1982. In 1983 he had another hit, the movie *Mr. Mom*. Since then he has scored with the blockbusters *Batman* and *Beetlejuice*. A good conversation starter with Keaton would be his less-than-successful television work. In 1979 he starred in the sitcom *Working Stiffs,* which lasted all of three weeks. In 1982, he starred in another sitcom, *Report to Murphy*, which did much better, lasting a full three months before being cancelled. Keaton's real name is Michael Douglas, but he changed it so he wouldn't be confused with the successful actor with the same name. He was born September 9, 1951, in Pittsburgh. Keaton is very open to pictures and autographs. He also has no problem talking with the public. Rating: 8.

## John F. Kennedy Jr.

John F. Kennedy Jr., was born into fame. His first home was the White House. His parents, the then-president of the United States John F. Kennedy and Jacqueline Kennedy, were the first couple to raise a baby in the White House since the 1800s. He is said to have an on-again, off-again relationship with actress Daryl Hannah. Kennedy graduated from New York University Law School and worked for the New York District Attorney. A good conversation starter with John might be his use as a major plot point in an episode of the television show *Seinfeld* (Elaine kept trying to meet him at a gym. Kennedy did not actually appear in the show). John was born in Washington, D.C., on November 25, 1960. He spends a lot of time in public and is very gracious to people who approach him. Rating: 8.

## Val Kilmer

Val Kilmer became famous when he starred in the hit movie *Top Secret* in 1984. He has gone on to star in the blockbuster *Top Gun* with Tom Cruise, and as Elvis Presley in *True Romance*, with Christian Slater. He also was excellent as Doc Holiday in *Tombstone* (a great line had him saying "I'm your huckleberry"). A good conversation starter with Val would be his role in the latest *Batman*, taking over for Michael Keaton. Val was born in Los Angeles, on December 31, 1959. He is very down-to-earth and doesn't really view himself as a star. I was on a airplane flight once with Val and Paul McCartney. The airline upgraded Val's ticket from coach to first class, and when they told Val he would be sitting near McCartney, he got almost giddy—he was so excited about meeting Paul. He is always friendly to the public and willing to take pictures and sign autographs. Rating: 9.

## Stephen King

Stephen King is one of the most successful novelists of all time. Since he released *Carrie* in 1974, he has topped the bestseller lists continuously. Some of his most famous books include *The Shining*, *Cujo*, *Christine*, *Pet Sematary*, and *Misery*. A good conversation starter with King could be the movie *The Running Man*. King decided to prove to himself that his books were so good they would sell without his very famous name attached, so he released *The Running Man* under the pen name Richard Bachman. A very astute film producer, George Linder, recognized the work as exceptional, although he had no idea King had written it. Linder began developing the film and only later found out that King had penned the novel. The movie went on to be a great success for Linder, King, and the film's star, Arnold Schwarzenegger. Stephen King was born in Portland, Maine, on September 21, 1947. He attends book signings and conventions and is therefore easy to find. He is usually pretty good about pictures and autographs. Rating: 6.

## Greg Kinnear

Greg Kinnear became famous as the host of E! television's hit show *Talk Soup*. Greg would show viewers the best clips from the day's episodes of talk shows. He was such a success that he was given his own network television show, taking over the reigns of *Later* from Bob Costas, and has been making a huge impact with his clever interviews. A good conversation starter with Greg would be his Fox television show *The Best of the Worst*, on which he celebrated the dumb and ridiculous things in life. Greg was born in Logansport, Indiana, in 1964. He is a lot of fun to meet because of his quick wit and great sense of humor. He is always happy to oblige the requests of the public, including pictures and autographs. Rating: 9.

## Nastassia Kinski

Nastassia Kinski gained fame when she starred in Roman Polanski's 1979 film *Tess*. She went on to star in *Cat People*, *Paris, Texas*, and, more recently, *Terminal Velocity* with Charlie Sheen. A good conversation starter with Nastassia would be her relationship with music producer Quincy Jones, with whom she has a child. Nastassia was born in Germany on January 24, 1959. She is moderately accessible, although it is difficult to find her out in public very often. Rating: 5.

## *Don Knotts*

You don't get any bigger in the world of entertainment than Don Knotts. Don stepped into the limelight with his unforgettable performance as deputy sheriff Barney Fife on the *Andy Griffith Show*. Knotts appeared on the show from 1960 through 1965 and owned the Emmy Award category for Outstanding Performance in a Supporting Role by an Actor or Actress in a Comedy Series during that entire time. He collected five Emmys for his work as the irrepressible Barney Fife. Don continued to blaze a legendary trail in television. In 1970 he debuted the *Don Knotts Show* on NBC, which ran for one incredible season, producing hilarious comedy bits such as the running skit about how difficult it was to put on the *Don Knotts Show*. This was groundbreaking material, and was the forerunner for some of today's biggest television hits, including the *Larry Sanders Show* and *Home Improvement*, which both use the "show within a show" premise. Don went on to create one of the most memorable characters ever to grace the television screen—Ralph Furley. From 1979 through 1984, Knotts played Furley on the television hit *Three's Company*. His clothing, antics, and comedy on that show have never been matched. While he has done other television, with just as memorable results (check out his performance as Les Calhoun on *Matlock*), his television work pales when compared to his unbelievable feature-film performances. In 1964, he was *The Incredible Mr. Limpet*. In 1966, he brought us the classic *The Ghost and Mr. Chicken*. Other classics followed, including *The Shakiest Gun in the West*, *The Love God?*, *Herbie Goes to Monte Carlo*, *Hot Lead, Cold Feet*, and the legendary *The Apple Dumpling Gang*. Generations from now, when historians look back at the biggest entertainment contributors, Don Knotts will surely emerge as the biggest star ever to work in show business. Don was born in Morgantown, West Virginia, on July 21, 1924. When it comes to meeting celebrities, you can't meet a more gracious human being than Don Knotts. Taking into consideration everyone that Steve and I have met, Knotts ranks at the very top of the list. He will go to any lengths to accommodate his fans. He will sit and talk for hours or sign autographs until the pen runs out of ink. If you have the good fortune to meet the legendary Don Knotts, please say hi for Steve and me. Rating: 10+.

## Ted Koppel

Ted Koppel has been covering the news since his early twenties. When he was twenty-three, he was hired by ABC as a television reporter. In 1975, at age thirty-five, he began hosting ABC's weekend news show. In 1980, Koppel became the anchor of *Nightline*, which has become one of the most respected news programs on the air. A good conversation starter with Koppel would be the dummy that was created in his likeness for the television show *D.C. Follies*. He was born in England on February 8, 1940. Ted is very accessible and is happy to talk with the public. He will also sign autographs and take pictures. Rating: 9.

## Ricki Lake

Ricki Lake debuted in movies in the cult classic *Hairspray*, with Sonny Bono and Pia Zadora. She was nineteen at the time. In 1993, she launched the talk show *Ricki Lake*, which has shot up like a rocket in the ratings. She is appealing to a wide range of demographics, and is especially popular with the younger crowd. She has created a show that is hip and creative. A good conversation starter with Ricki would be her role as Holly the Donut Dolly on the hit television series *China Beach*. Ricki was born in New York on September 21, 1968. She is exceptionally accessible and is very "into" her fans and the public. She is happy to sign autographs and take pictures. Rating: 9.

## John Larroquette

John Larroquette has been involved in many successful projects, but he garnered the most attention as Dan Fielding on the hit television show *Night Court*. In fact, he won four consecutive Emmy Awards for that role. John was also a regular on the television show *Baa Baa Black Sheep* with Robert Conrad. He has appeared in movies, too, most notably in the classic film *Stripes* with Bill Murray—Larroquette was the star of the famous loofah scene. John was born in New Orleans on November 25, 1947. Every time Steve and I have met John we have ended up discussing *Stripes*, which is one of our favorite movies. John is a lot of fun to talk to and always obliges requests for autographs and pictures. Rating: 8.

# Joey Lawrence

Joey Lawrence is best known as Joey Russo on the hit television series *Blossom*. Joey has been on *Blossom* since it began in early 1991. He is a regular on the teen gossip magazine covers and always draws screams from the young girls waiting outside awards shows. A good conversation starter with Joey would be his role as Joey Donovan on the television series *Gimme a Break*. Joey was born in Montgomery, Pennsylvania, on April 20, 1976. He is very aware of the career support he gets from his fans and is always willing to take pictures and sign autographs. Rating: 8.

# Jay Leno

Jay Leno is the very popular host of the *Tonight* show, which he took over from Johnny Carson in 1992. Leno began as a stand-up comic and played all of the famous clubs around the country. Today he sells out show after show in the main showroom at Caesar's Palace in Las Vegas. His original style of comedy is hilarious, and his policy of staying away from blue material is refreshing. Jay gained national exposure when his friend David Letterman started booking him regularly on *Late Night With David Letterman*. Leno became the regular guest-host of the *Tonight* show after Joan Rivers left the position. Then, when Carson retired in 1992, Leno took over. A good conversation starter with Jay would be anything about cars or motorcycles, as he is an avid collector. Jay was born James Leno in New Rochelle, New York, on April 28, 1950. He is one of the most accessible celebrities. Even with a bad opening line, Jay will jump right into a conversation. He has a great rapport with the public and is happy to sign autographs and take pictures. Rating: 9.

# David Letterman

David Letterman is currently the host of the *Late Show With David Letterman*. In 1982 Letterman debuted his original show *Late Night*

*With David Letterman* on NBC. It quickly became one of the best shows on television. Letterman's unique style and slant on things struck home with millions of viewers. He introduced the world to such characters as Larry "Bud" Melman and to such program features such as Stupid Pet Tricks and the Top Ten List. In 1992, Letterman was passed over for the job of hosting the *Tonight* show when Johnny Carson retired. Because of the way the situation was handled, Letterman decided to pack up his show and go elsewhere. He landed at CBS, opposite *Tonight*, with one of the most lucrative contracts in television history. Since he unveiled his newly titled *Late Show With David Letterman* on CBS, it has gotten better and better. Letterman is clearly at the top of his game. A good conversation starter with Dave would be his early job as a TV weatherman. He once congratulated a tropical storm for being upgraded to a hurricane, on the air. David was born in Indianapolis, Indiana, on April 12, 1947. If you're looking for a fun time, meet David Letterman. His humor is contagious. After five minutes of talking with Dave, you feel like you're having the time of your life. He is a terrific personality. Dave is happy to sign autographs and take pictures. Steve and I have met Dave four or five times and have never been let down. Rating: 9.

## Al Lewis

Al Lewis is best known as Grandpa Munster on the television show *The Munsters*. He looked like an old Dracula and bungled around his laboratory. Al also starred on *Car 54—Where are You?*. A good conversation starter with Al would be the expletive-filled oration on free speech he gave in support of radio talk show legend Howard Stern. Al was born Alexander Meister in New York on April 30, 1923. He is fairly accessible and will usually sign autographs. Occasionally, he is a little ornery. Rating: 5.

## Jerry Lewis

Jerry Lewis originally was best known as half of the Dean Martin-Jerry Lewis comedy team that made many hit movies. Lately, he is probably most identified with his work on behalf of muscular dystrophy. His telethon every Labor Day weekend has become an American tradition. In the movies, Martin and Lewis teamed up for ten years and over ten films. The two then split, and Lewis began making hits on his own, including *The Sad Sack*, *The Bellboy*, *The Nutty Professor*, and *Don't Give Up the Ship*. His career slowed after a few tries at television, until he turned in an incredible performance in the 1983 film *King of Comedy* with Robert De Niro. A good conversation starter with Jerry would be his role as a garment industry bigshot on the television series *Wiseguy* with Ken Wahl. Jerry was born Joseph Levitch in Newark, New Jersey, on March 16, 1926. He is a little difficult to approach. Jerry has been in show business a long time and seems a little tired of the attention that goes along with being a star. Rating: 4.

# Jerry Lee Lewis

Jerry Lee Lewis is one of the pioneers of rock and roll. He was one of the original inductees into the Rock and Roll Hall of Fame, along with Elvis Presley, Little Richard, and Chuck Berry. One of Jerry Lee's biggest hits is "Great Balls of Fire." A good conversation starter would be the time Jerry was arrested after crashing his car into the famed music gates in front of Graceland, Elvis Presley's home. He was quoted as saying he was there to kill Elvis, but he later said he was only joking. Jerry Lee was born in Ferriday, Louisiana, on September 29, 1935. He is in the middle of the road as far as accessibility. It certainly isn't easy to strike up a conversation with him, but if you come up with the right angle, it can be done. Rating: 4.

# Christopher Lloyd

Christopher Lloyd became famous as Jim Ignatowski on the hit television show *Taxi*. Lloyd appeared on *Taxi* from 1979 until the show was cancelled in 1983. His success on *Taxi* jump-started his movie career. In 1985, he starred in the blockbuster *Back to the Future* with Michael J. Fox, and also starred in the 1989 and 1990 sequels. Lloyd has also been in the movies *Star Trek III: The Search for Spock* and *The Addams Family*. A good conversation starter for Christopher would be his strong performance in his film debut, as a mental patient in *One Flew Over the Cuckoo's Nest*. Lloyd was born in Stamford, Connecticut, on October 22, 1938. He

Steve with *Melrose Place* star Heather Locklear

is a very funny guy and entertaining to meet. He is happy to sign autographs and take pictures. Rating: 7.

## Heather Locklear

Heather Locklear seems to have the magic touch when it comes to television. She has been in four television series, and three have been huge hits. She starred as Sammy Jo Dean on the popular television show *Dynasty*. She also played Officer Stacy Sheridan on the police show *T. J. Hooker* with William Shatner. Currently she is the very popular star of the hit television show *Melrose Place*. A good conversation starter with Heather would be her husband, Bon Jovi guitarist Richie Sambora, or her only short-lived television project, *Going Places*. Heather was born in Los Angeles, on September 25, 1961. She is happy to talk with the public. The few times we have met her she was more than willing to take pictures and sign autographs. Rating: 8.

## Jack Lord

Jack Lord secured his claim to fame as Detective Steve McGarrett on the classic police drama *Hawaii Five-O*. Week after week, millions of viewers tuned in to hear Jack say, "Book 'em, Danno." A good conversation starter with Jack would be his appearance on the 1956 television show *Conflict*. Jack's real name is Jack Ryan. He was born in New York City on December 30, 1930. Jack is a very gracious man and is happy to meet with the public. He will sign autographs and take pictures. Rating: 7.

## Julia Louis-Dreyfus

Julia Louis-Dreyfus has hit the big time as Elaine Benes on the hit television series *Seinfeld*. Before *Seinfeld*, Julia was a regular on *Saturday Night Live* from 1982 through 1985. She also had a short run as one of the stars of *Day by Day*, a sitcom that lasted less than a year. A good conversation starter with Julia would be the fact that she worked with her husband while on *Saturday Night Live*. His name is Brad Hall and he was a member of *SNL* from 1982 through 1984. Julia was born in New York on January 13, 1961. She is happy to sign autographs and take pictures. The few times Steve and I met her, she was always in a very good mood. Rating: 7.

## Jon Lovitz

Jon Lovitz gained national attention as a cast member of *Saturday Night Live*. He was a regular on the program from 1985 through 1990. He had a number of stand-out characters, including Tommy Flanagan, the pathological liar ("Yeah, that's the ticket!"). Lovitz has since gone on to feature films, where he usually is found in a supporting role. His portrayal of a talent scout in *A League of Their Own* won him a lot of attention. A good conversation starter with Jon would be the voice-over work he did on *The Simpsons* or his new show *The Critic*. Lovitz was born in Tarzana, California, on July 21, 1957. He is approachable to a point. He seems open to taking pictures and signing autographs, but sometimes doesn't seem too happy about it. Rating: 6.

## Susan Lucci

In 1969, Susan Lucci joined the cast of the daytime soap opera *All My Children*. She has been the star of the show ever since, and, in fact, is one of the most popular soap stars of all time. She has been nominated over a dozen times for an Emmy Award for her performance in "All My Children"; but she has lost every time. A good conversation starter with Susan would be her role on the hit television series *Dallas* during the 1990–1991 season. Susan was born in Scarsdale, New York, on December 23, 1948. She is very friendly in person and has no problem taking pictures and signing autographs. You will have no problem striking up a conversation with her. Rating: 8.

## Gavin MacLeod

Gavin MacLeod is the most famous cruise ship captain of all time. For nine years he was captain of the *Love Boat*, on the hit television series on ABC. Gavin also played Murray Slaughter on the *Mary Tyler Moore Show*. A good conversation starter with Gavin would be his role of spokesman for Princess Cruise Lines, or his role as Happy Haines on *McHale's Navy*. Gavin was born in Mt. Kisco, New York, on February 28, 1931. He is approachable in public and is usually happy to sign autographs and take pictures. Rating: 7.

## Madonna

Madonna is one of the most successful female singers of all time. She broke into the big leagues in 1984, and has almost constantly been at or near the top of the charts since then. She has hit the pop charts numerous times, with songs that include "Like a Virgin," "Lucky Star," "Holiday," and "Borderline." Madonna released a documentary in 1991, entitled *Truth or Dare*. She broke into movies in 1985, starring in *Desperately Seeking Susan*, and has been in a number of films since then. A good conversation starter with Madonna would be her strong portrayal of a baseball player in *A League of Their Own*. Madonna was born Madonna Louise Veronica Ciccone in Bay City, Michigan, on August 16, 1959. Madonna is very difficult to approach. She is whisked around by handlers and definitely is used to the star treatment. Rating: 3.

# John Malkovich

John Malkovich has made a name for himself as a very intense film actor. His debut film was *The Killing Fields* in 1984. Later in 1984, he earned an Academy Award nomination for his role in *Places in the Heart*. He has starred in some major Hollywood hits, such as *In the Line of Fire* with Clint Eastwood. A good conversation starter would be the fact that he helped found the Steppenwolf Theater Company in Chicago. John was born in Benton, Illinois, on December 9, 1953. He is fairly accessible and usually will sign autographs and take pictures. Rating: 6.

# Steve Martin

Steve Martin is one of the most successful comedy actors ever. He has made many films that are classics in the comedy genre. His first starring role was in *The Jerk* in 1979, a film that placed among the top three money-makers that year. Since then he has starred in many of my personal favorite movies, including *Planes, Trains, and Automobiles* with John Candy, *Leap of Faith* with Debra Winger, and *The Man With Two Brains*. Before going into movies Steve Martin was a hugely successful stand-up comedian. A good conversation starter with Steve would be the fact that one of his first jobs was playing the banjo at Disneyland. Steve was born in Waco, Texas, on August 14, 1945. He is very difficult to approach. If you ask him for an autograph he hands you a card that says, "You just met Steve Martin." Rating: 3.

# Walter Matthau

Walter Matthau first made a significant impact playing Elvis Presley's adversary in the 1956 movie *King Creole*. Matthau went on to star in some major hits, including *The Odd Couple* and *The Bad News Bears*. A good conversation starter with Matthau would be his appearance on the television drama the *Alcoa Hour* in the 1950s. The *Alcoa Hour* was one of the best drama shows of the era. Matthau was born Walter Matasschanskayasky in New York City on October 1, 1920. While I have never seen him turn down an autograph or picture request, he never seems too happy about it. Rating: 5.

## Paul McCartney

Paul McCartney is one of the most prolific songwriters ever. He was, of course, a member of the Beatles. As a Beatle, McCartney reached the top of the pop charts twenty times, with such hits as "I Want to Hold Your Hand," "Help!," "Yesterday," "Hey Jude," and "Let It Be." He left the Beatles and started Wings with his wife Linda. Wings hit the number one spot six times, with songs that included "Band on the Run" and "Listen to What the Man Said." A good conversation starter with Paul would be the school he started in Liverpool. McCartney is very difficult to approach. He is whisked around by handlers very quickly. When Steve and I met him, he had shown up at a radio station to do an interview. He drove up in a Corvette with a manager and was followed by two limousines. After McCartney went inside, I asked one of the limo drivers why he had followed McCartney, since Paul was driving himself. He told me that he was there just in case McCartney's Corvette broke down. I asked what the purpose of the second limo was, and he replied that the second limo was just in case McCartney's Corvette *and* the first limo both broke down. McCartney and his people take no chances that Paul will have to mill around, even for a minute. Rating: 3.

## John Mellencamp

John Mellencamp first became famous as John Cougar. His album *American Fool* produced many hit singles, including the number one hit "Jack and Diane." After the success of his first album, John released his next album under the name John Cougar Mellencamp. These days he is simply John Mellencamp. John has had many hits over the past ten years, including "Rain on the Scarecrow" and "Pink Houses." A good conversation starter with John would be anything about his paintings— he is a very accomplished artist. John was born in Seymour, Indiana, on October 7, 1951. He is very personable, likes meeting the public, and has no problem signing autographs or taking pictures. Rating: 8.

## Dennis Miller

Dennis Miller attained national stardom as the host of the news segment on *Saturday Night Live*. His news parodies were hilarious, always end-ing with his trademark phrase, "And I am outta here!!" Dennis went on to host a late-night talk show that didn't last very long. He is currently hosting a weekly comedy show for HBO. A good conversation starter for Dennis would be his early show business break on Ed McMahon's *Star Search*. Dennis was born in Pittsburgh on November 3, 1953. Steve and I have met Dennis three times. Two times he was in a foul mood, and the other time he was jovial enough to take pictures with us and talk for a few minutes before saying, "It's too cold out here, I'm going back in." Good luck approaching Dennis. Rating: 4.

## Demi Moore

Demi Moore's biggest film to date is *Ghost*, with Patrick Swayze. She has also starred in *Indecent Proposal* with Robert Redford and Woody Harrelson, as well as in *A Few Good Men* with Tom Cruise and Jack Nicholson. A good conversation starter with Demi would be her early stint on the daytime soap opera *General Hospital*, or her husband, actor Bruce Willis. Demi's real name is Demetria Guynes. She was born November 11, 1962, in Roswell, New Mexico. Demi is very sweet and is happy to meet the public. She is very funny and you will have a great conversation. She is also willing to sign autographs and take pictures. Look for her at the openings of new Planet Hollywood locations. Rating: 8.

## Dudley Moore

Dudley Moore is well known for two famous movies. His first hit was *10*, with Bo Derek, and his second was *Arthur* in which he played a lovable drunk. Dudley has starred in a dozen other films, and has been quite good in most, but he is still remembered for those two films. A good conversation starter with Dudley would be his piano-playing. He is an accomplished talent. Dudley was born in England on April 19, 1935. He is very funny in person and is very approachable. He is happy to take pictures and sign autographs. Rating: 7.

## Mary Tyler Moore

Mary Tyler Moore hit the big time in two television series. First, she was featured as Laura Petrie on the *Dick Van Dyke Show* from 1961 through 1966. In 1970, she hit again with the *Mary Tyler Moore Show*, which ran until 1977 and was a huge ratings champion. Mary has also starred in many feature films. In 1980, she earned an Academy Award nomination for her performance in *Ordinary People*. Back in 1969 she starred with Elvis Presley in *Change of Habit*. A good conversation starter with Mary would be her producing credits on such television hits as *Hill Street Blues* and *St. Elsewhere*. Mary was born in New York on December 29, 1937. She is not very talkative when approached, but she will sign autographs and take pictures. Rating: 6.

## Donny Most

Donny Most has not appeared in many entertainment projects, but his one standout reserves his place in celebrity history. From 1974 through 1980, Donny Most played Ralph Malph on the hit television series *Happy Days*. Donny was born in New York on August 8, 1953. He is very outgoing, loves to talk to the public, and is happy to sign autographs and take pictures. Rating: 8.

## Eddie Murphy

Eddie Murphy graduated from the cast of *Saturday Night Live* after a three-year run (1981–1984) to become one of Hollywood's biggest box office draws. In 1982 he was in the blockbuster *48 Hours*. In 1983 he was in another hit, *Trading Places* with Dan Aykroyd. Then, in 1984, his status as a huge box office draw was solidified with the release of *Beverly Hills Cop*. A good conversation starter with Eddie would be the memorabilia room he has set up in his house as a tribute to Elvis Presley—Eddie owns one of the capes that Elvis used to wear in concert. Eddie was born in New York on April 3, 1961. He is difficult to approach since he travels with a large entourage that tries to keep people away. Rating: 4.

## Bill Murray

Bill Murray became famous as one of the big stars of *Saturday Night Live*. Bill was on *SNL* for three years, from 1977 to 1980. In 1979,

Bret and Steve with *Coach* star Craig T. Nelson

Murray appeared in the comedy classic *Meatballs*, which is one of the funniest movies ever made. He followed up *Meatballs* with the 1980 hit *Caddyshack*. In 1981, he was in another movie that will go down in history as one of the top-ten comedy films, *Stripes*, with John Candy and Harold Ramis. More recent films starring Murray include the hits *Groundhog Day*, *What About Bob?*, and *Mad Dog and Glory*. A good conversation starter with Bill would be baseball. He's a big fan. Additionally, you could talk with him about Howard Cosell, who gave Bill his first big break on *Saturday Night Live With Howard Cosell*. Bill was born in Wilmette, Illinois, on September 21, 1950. He is not very interested in taking pictures or signing autographs. Occasionally, you can catch him in a generous mood. Rating: 6.

## Craig T. Nelson

Craig T. Nelson is best known as the head coach of Minnesota State University's Screaming Eagles football team on the television series *Coach*. Craig has been playing Coach Hayden Fox since 1989 when the series debuted on ABC. Nelson has also appeared in many feature films, including *Poltergeist*, *The Killing Fields*, and *Action Jack-*

*son*. A good conversation starter for Craig would be his love of race cars. He competes in the celebrity race at the Long Beach Grand Prix. Nelson was born in Spokane, Washington, on April 4, 1946. He is very funny and great to meet; happy to sit around and talk, or sign autographs and take pictures. Rating: 8.

## Bob Newhart

Bob Newhart is one of the most successful television actors ever. He has been the star of two of the highest rated series in television history. In 1972, he debuted the *Bob Newhart Show* on CBS and the show went through the roof, finally leaving the air toward the end of 1978. Bob played a psychologist whose patients were "interesting." In 1982, Bob was back, and in a big way. His new show, simply titled *Newhart*, became an instant success. This time Bob was the proprietor of the Stratford Inn, a historical inn located in Vermont. *Newhart* was a ratings champion throughout its run, which finally ended in 1990. Bob ended both of these shows while they were still at the top of the ratings. A good conversation starter with Bob would be his appearances with the legendary Don Adams on the *Don Adams Screen Test*. Bob was born George Robert Newhart in Chicago on September 5, 1929. Bob is generally approachable. He is willing to take pictures and sign autographs. Rating: 7.

## Paul Newman

Paul Newman won the Academy Award for Best Actor for his performance in the 1986 Martin Scorsese film *The Color of Money*. The year before, he was awarded an honorary Oscar for his incredible body of work, which included six Academy Award nominations. Paul's films include many classics, such as *Hud*, *The Hustler*, *Cool Hand Luke*, *Butch Cassidy and the Sundance Kid*, and *The Sting*. A good conversation starter with Paul would be his dedicated work for charity. He has a line of salad dressings, popcorn, and other food items, from which he donates every penny of profit to charity. Paul was born in Cleveland on January 29, 1925. He is one of the true legends work-

Bret with Jack Nicholson (Candice Bergen in background)

ing today. Despite his huge popularity, he is very approachable and has no problem signing autographs and taking pictures. Rating: 8.

## Jack Nicholson

Jack Nicholson gained national prominence with an Academy Award–nominated performance in the 1969 film *Easy Rider*. Although he had made dozens of low-budget films previously and had appeared in a handful of television shows, *Easy Rider* was a turning point for Jack. He went on to be a major box office attraction. His credits include the films *One Flew Over the Cuckoo's Nest*, *Terms of Endearment*, *Chinatown*, *Goin' South*, *Prizzi's Honor*, *Batman*, and *A Few Good Men*. One scene for which he is well known is when he says, "Heeere's Johnny!!" in *The Shining*. A good conversation starter with Jack would be the Los Angeles Lakers basketball team, of which he is a huge fan. Another topic would be his early job as a messenger at the MGM studios. Jack was born in Neptune, New Jersey, on April 22, 1937. He is one of the most obnoxious celebrities Steve and I have ever met. The few times we have seen him in public, he seems to walk around like he is God's gift to the world. He is rather unapproachable and usually will not take pictures or sign autographs. Rating: 2.

## Conan O'Brien

In 1992 Conan O'Brien took over the time slot vacated by David Letterman at NBC. He has quickly gained a huge following with his show *Late Night With Conan O'Brien*. Conan had big shoes to fill, trying to pick up the slack after Letterman's departure to CBS, and was given almost no chance to succeed. But succeed he did, and in a huge way. At a time when talk show hosts come and go, Conan's quick wit and on-screen charisma have created a winning show that will be around for a long time. Conan began in show business as a writer, creating classic scenes for *Saturday Night Live* and *The Simpsons*. A good conversation starter with Conan would be his Harvard University education. Conan was born in Brookline, Massachusetts, on April 18, 1963. He is very approachable and gracious. He loves to talk with the public and has no problem signing autographs and taking pictures. Rating: 9.

## Ed O'Neill

Ed O'Neill is the comic genius who brings the world shoe salesman Al Bundy on the hit television series *Married . . . With Children*. In 1994, *Married . . . With Children* became the longest-running television sitcom currently on the air. When the Fox network debuted in 1987, *Married . . . With Children* was in the lineup, and it was Fox's first major hit. Ed has also done a number of movies, including *Ford Fairlane* with Andrew "Dice" Clay, and *Dutch* with Ethan Randall. Ed was born on April 12, 1946, in Youngstown, Ohio. He is very approachable and has no problem with autographs or pictures. Rating: 8.

## Al Pacino

Al Pacino finally won a Best Actor Oscar for his performance in the 1992 film *Scent of a Woman*. His place in movie history was already solidified by his long list of highly acclaimed films and Academy Award nominations. Some of Al's most memorable films include *The Godfather* (and its two sequels), *Dog Day Afternoon*, *Serpico*, *. . . And Justice for All*, *Scarface*, and *Carlito's Way*. A good conversation starter with Al would be stage acting. Al is very accomplished and loves theater. He is currently working on a Shakespeare documentary. Al was born in New York City on April 25, 1940. His full name is Alfredo James Pacino. Al is a little difficult to approach. Being an acting legend, he is constantly being approached and he seems a little annoyed at the nonstop attention. Rating: 4.

## Sarah Jessica Parker

Sarah Jessica Parker recently became a huge star after her role in the blockbuster movie *Honeymoon in Vegas* with Nicolas Cage. The year before, she gained a lot of attention in *L.A. Story* with Steve Martin. She has since starred in a number of films, including *Striking Distance* with Bruce Willis, *Ed Wood* with Johnny Depp, and *Miami Rhapsody* with Mia Farrow. A good conversation starter with Sarah would be her role in the television sitcom *Square Pegs* at the age of seventeen. Sarah was born in Nelsonville, Ohio, on March 25, 1965. She is very approachable. Sarah is very gracious with the public and has no problem signing autographs or taking pictures. Rating: 8.

## Dolly Parton

Dolly Parton is best known as a very successful country music singer. She has had many hit songs, including "Here You Come Again" and "Nine to Five." She has also had a formidable movie career, which includes the hit *Nine to Five*, the critically-acclaimed *Steel Magnolias*, as well as *Rhinestone* with Sylvester Stallone. Dolly has also appeared on television. She had her own variety show, *Dolly*, in the late eighties on ABC. A good conversation starter with Dolly would be her amusement park, Dollywood. Dolly was born in Sevierville, Tennessee, on January 19, 1946. She is very nice to the public and you will have no trouble initiating a conversation with her, having her sign autographs, or pose for pictures. Rating: 8.

## Sean Penn

Sean Penn is best known as a movie actor. However, his relationship with Madonna and his headline-grabbing run-ins with the press have also kept him in the spotlight. Sean has turned in many strong film performances, including *Carlito's Way* with Al Pacino, and *Taps* with Tom Cruise. My favorite Penn film had him playing a spaced-out teenage surfer in *Fast Times at Ridgemont High*, with Phoebe Cates. A good conversation starter with Sean could be his brother Chris, who has also had a career in the movies. Sean was born in Burbank, California, on August 17, 1960. Steve and I met Sean only once, backstage at a Madonna concert, and he was extremely gracious. Sean has the reputation of hating cameramen, the press, and autograph hounds. So our experience says that he is approachable, and his reputation says, be careful how you try. Rating: 5.

## Luke Perry

Luke Perry became famous as Dylan McKay on the hit television series *Beverly Hills 90210*. He has starred on that show since its beginning in 1990, and his role has made him the cover story of many teen fan magazines. A good conversation starter with Luke would be his one-year role on the daytime soap opera *Loving*. Luke was born Coy Luther Perry III on October 11, 1965, in Fredericktown, Ohio. Luke is very open to the public and his fans. He is happy to take pictures and sign autographs. You will have no trouble approaching Luke. Rating: 8.

## Joe Pesci

Joe Pesci has had a lot of success through the years as a feature-film actor. In 1980, he was nominated for Best Supporting Actor for his performance in *Raging Bull* with Robert De Niro. In 1990, he turned in a great performance in *GoodFellas*. His other hits include *Home Alone*, *Lethal Weapon*, and the Academy Award–winning *My Cousin Vinny*. A good conversation starter with Joe would be his starring role in *Half Nelson*, the short-lived television show with Dick Butkus, Bubba Smith, and Dean Martin. Joe was born in Newark, New Jersey, on February 9, 1943. He is very outgoing and fun to meet, happy to talk with the public, sign autographs, and take pictures. Rating: 7.

## Michelle Pfeiffer

Michelle Pfeiffer is recognized as one of the best actresses working, but I have no idea why. Most of her films have been disappointments, including *Grease 2*, *Charlie Chan and the Curse of the Dragon Queen*, *Ladyhawke*, *Into the Night*, and even the 1994 big-budget Jack Nicholson film *Wolf*. The success of films that she has been in usually has had little to do with her. She was merely window dressing in the 1983 hit *Scarface* with Al Pacino; *The Witches of Eastwick* featured a number of huge stars, including Jack Nicholson, Cher, and Susan Sarandon, so Michelle didn't have to carry the movie; and *Batman* was a huge hit before she appeared in the sequel. Michelle was born in Santa Ana, California, on April 29, 1958. I am worried that my review of Pfeiffer's work might be slanted, based on the fact that all four times Steve and I have met her, she walked around with her nose in the air, very full of herself. We have seen her tell many people, "No, I don't *do* pictures." She is very much aware of her star status and seems to feel that people owe her, and not the other way around. Rating: 1.

## Regis Philbin

Regis is one of the most successful talk show hosts of all time. As the star of *Live With Regis and Kathie Lee*, he has redefined the standard for talk shows. His comedy and interview style are unmatched, and his show is hilarious day in and day out. Regis's first big break came as host of the *A.M. Los Angeles* show, which he hosted for seven years. He then became successful as the host of the *Morning Show* in New York in 1983. Regis has been very successful with each of his talk shows, and his career shows no sign of letting up any time soon. A good conversation starter with Regis would be his work as a page for the *Tonight* show. Regis was born in New York on August 25, 1934. He was named after his father's high school. Regis is one of the nicest people you will ever meet. He is very funny in person and your conversation with him is always entertaining. He is

Bret with Brad Pitt

very accessible and loves to talk with the public, is happy to sign autographs, and will take pictures. Rating: 9.

## Brad Pitt

Brad Pitt has become one of the hottest young actors working today. With such films as *Kalifornia*, *Cool World*, and *Johnny Suede*, he had begun to be recognized not only as very talented, but also as a box office draw. In 1992, he turned in a stellar performance in Robert Redford's *And a River Runs Through It*. Recently he has starred in *Interview with the Vampire* with Tom Cruise, and in *Legends of the Fall*. A good conversation starter with Brad would be his cameo in *True Romance* as Elvis Presley, or his having been voted 1994's Sexiest Man in America by *People* magazine. Brad was born in Shawnee, Oklahoma, on December 18, 1963. He is very accessible and is happy to take pictures and sign autographs. Rating: 8.

## Jason Priestley

Jason Priestley is best known as Brandon Walsh on the hit television show *Beverly Hills 90210*. He has been starring in the series since

Bret with former president Ronald Reagan

it began on the Fox network in 1990. Jason also appeared in the television series *Sister Kate*, as well as in *21 Jump Street*. He recently starred in his first feature film, *Calendar Girl*, in which he is trying to get a date with the legendary Marilyn Monroe. A good conversation starter with Jason would be hockey, as he is an avid fan. He also plays the sport and can be found skating for the T. J. Martell Charity during celebrity hockey games. Jason was born in Canada on August 28, 1969. He is very approachable and you will have no trouble starting a conversation with him—usually you just have to say hello. He is willing to sign autographs or take pictures with anyone who asks. Rating: 8.

## Ronald Reagan

Ronald Reagan was the fortieth president of the United States. He took office in 1981, after beating Jimmy Carter in the presidential election. He left office in 1989, turning over the presidency to his vice president, George Bush. He was one of the most popular presidents of all time, leaving office with an approval rating in the 90 percent range. He was also the governor of California. Mr. Reagan began his career as an actor and starred in a number of feature films, as well as the television series *Death Valley Days*. A good conversation starter with Mr. Reagan would be anything about horses, as he is a very accomplished rider. He was born in Tampico, Illinois, on February 6, 1911. Mr. Reagan is protected by the Secret Service, so he is difficult to approach. I met Mr. Reagan recently and he and his people are exceedingly gracious. Rating: 7.

## Robert Redford

Robert Redford has always been considered one of the top movie actors working today, and he has added to those praises as a film director. The classic films in which he appears include *Butch Cassidy and the Sundance Kid*, *All the President's Men*, *The Natural*, and *The Sting*. His first directing effort, *Ordinary People* earned him an Academy Award for Best Director. A good conversation starter with Robert would be his Sundance Film Festival, which is becoming the premier film festival in the United States. Redford was born Charles Robert Redford, Jr., in Santa Monica, California, on August 18, 1937. Redford is very down-to-earth and is happy to meet and talk with the public. You usually won't have any trouble asking for autographs or pictures. Rating: 7.

## Keanu Reeves

Keanu Reeves gained national attention in the film *Bill and Ted's Excellent Adventure*. He went on to star in one of 1994's biggest money-makers, the action movie *Speed*. Keanu has been in a number of other films, including *Parenthood* with Steve Martin, and *Dangerous Liaisons* with Glenn Close, Michelle Pfeiffer, and John Malkovich. A good conversation starter with Keanu would be his first name. His mother, who is part Hawaiian, named him Keanu, which, loosely translated from Hawaiian, means "refreshing breeze." Keanu was born in Beirut, Lebanon, on September 2, 1964, and grew up in Canada. He is fairly approachable and is usually willing to sign autographs and take pictures. Rating: 6.

## Judge Reinhold

Judge Reinhold will never be forgotten as the star of the classic movie *Fast Times at Ridgemont High*. Almost as impressive was his role as a member of Bill Murray's platoon in the blockbuster *Stripes* (he wore the cool sweatshirt with the words, *Disco Sucks*). He has gone on to appear in the hit movies *Beverly Hills Cop* and its sequels, *Gremlins*, and *Ruthless People* with Danny DeVito. A good conversation starter with Judge would be his appearance on the hit television show *Seinfeld* as a "close talker," for which he won an Emmy nomination. Judge was born in Wilmington, Delaware, on May 21, 1957. He is very accessible, is great to talk to, and has some interesting stories about the filming of *Stripes*. He is happy to sign autographs and take pictures. Rating: 8.

## Paul Reiser

Paul Reiser has achieved superstardom as Paul Buchman on the television series *Mad About You* on NBC. Before *Mad About You*, Paul starred in another popular television sitcom, *My Two Dads*. Paul began his career in show business as a stand-up comedian. He has appeared in a number of hit feature films, including *Beverly Hills Cop* and *Aliens*. A good conversation starter with Paul would be his film debut in the movie *Diner* in 1982. Paul was born in New York City on March 30, 1957. He is fairly accessible, but sometimes is not interested in stopping to chat. He is very funny in person and if you catch him on a good day, you'll have a great time meeting him. Rating: 6.

## Burt Reynolds

Burt Reynolds has been very successful both on television and in the movies. He had major film hits with *The Longest Yard*, *Hooper*, *Smokey and the Bandit*, *The Cannonball Run*, and *The Best Little Whorehouse in Texas*. In the late 1980s Reynolds turned to television and starred in *B. L. Stryker*. In 1990 he debuted in the hit television series *Evening Shade*, with Marilu Henner. Burt created quite a few headlines with his split from his wife, Loni Anderson. A good conversation starter with Burt would be the short-lived television show, *Hawk*, in which he starred for four months in 1966. Burt was born in Waycross, Georgia, on February 11, 1936. He is very cordial in person and is usually happy to take pictures and sign autographs. Rating: 7.

Bret with *Seinfeld*'s Michael "Kramer" Richards

## Michael Richards

Michael Richards is best known as Kramer on the hit television show *Seinfeld*. Richards has become one of the most popular members of the cast and he has earned an Emmy for his terrific performances as Kramer. He was also in the television show *Fridays* in 1980. Larry David, who is the executive producer of *Seinfeld*, worked on *Fridays* with Richards. A good conversation starter with Richards would be his guest appearance on *Miami Vice*. Michael was born in Culver City, California, on July 14, 1950. He is very approachable and has no problem signing autographs or taking pictures. Rating: 8.

## Geraldo Rivera

Geraldo Rivera gained fame in 1972 as a hard-hitting investigative reporter, uncovering the indecent treatment of mental patients at the Willowbrook State School. This report helped change the way mental patients were treated throughout the country. In 1978, Rivera joined the ABC program *20/20* and increased his exposure as one of the top journalists in the country. He left the show in 1986 and went on to launch *Geraldo*, a daytime talk show that has been very successful. Geraldo is one of the top hosts, due to his creative style and hard-hitting topics. A good conversation starter with Geraldo would be his boxing match against Frank Stallone (Sylvester Stallone's brother) on the Howard Stern radio show. Geraldo was born in New York on July 4, 1943. He is very approachable and seems genuinely interested in conversations with the public. He is always happy to sign autographs and take pictures. Rating: 9.

## Joan Rivers

Joan Rivers is best known as the talk show host who first featured Steve and me. She has had a long and storied career. Her talk show, the *Joan Rivers Show*, was a huge success. She was also the guest-host on the *Tonight* show for many years and was one of the best ever to hold that role. She is a stand-up comic and has appeared in Las Vegas on a regular basis. A good conversation starter with Joan would be the fact that she was the permanent "center square" on the *Hollywood Squares* in 1987. Joan was born Joan Molinsky in New York on June 8, 1937. She is very accessible and is happy to talk with the public. She will also sign autographs. Rating: 8.

## Julia Roberts

Julia Roberts became the biggest female Hollywood box office draw after the 1990 release of *Pretty Woman*. She had turned in a great performance the year before in *Steel Magnolias*, and has gone on to play Tinkerbell in *Hook* and a lead role in the film version of John Grisham's novel *The Pelican Brief*. Julia is the sister of actor Eric Roberts. A good conversation starter with Julia would be her early ambition to become a veterinarian. Julia was born in Smyrna, Georgia, on October 28, 1967. She is fairly accessible and will usually sign autographs and take pictures. Rating: 7.

## Axl Rose

Axl Rose is best known as the lead singer of one of the biggest rock bands, Guns 'N' Roses. His first effort with the band was released in 1986. In 1987, Guns 'N' Roses released the album *Appetite for Destruction*, which sold over 15 million copies. *Appetite for Destruction* included the hit songs "Welcome to the Jungle" and "Sweet Child o'

Steve with Roseanne

Mine." In 1991, they released an unprecedented two albums at once: *Use Your Illusion I* and *Use Your Illusion II*. Both albums quickly shot to the number one and two positions on the sales charts. In 1993, the band released an album of punk cover songs, entitled *The Spaghetti Incident?* A good conversation starter with Axl would be the inclusion of a song written by Charles Manson on *The Spaghetti Incident?* The song is a hidden track that has no mention on the album cover, but if you play song 12, "I Don't Care About You," the Manson song follows. Axl legally changed his name to W. Axl Rose from William Bailey. He was born in Lafayette, Indiana. Axl will put up with requests for pictures and autographs. He was once charged by the police for attacking a fan who was taking pictures of him during a concert performance—so be careful. Rating: 5.

## Roseanne

Roseanne is best known as the star of the hit television comedy series *Roseanne* on ABC. She was a stand-up comic before she hit the big time with her top-rated series. She has also starred in the feature film *She Devil*, with Meryl Streep. Roseanne recently was in the headlines after her high-profile split with her husband, actor Tom Arnold. A good conversation starter with Roseanne would be her role as host of the

MTV Music Awards. She was born Roseanne Barr in Salt Lake City, Utah, on November 3, 1952. Roseanne is fairly accessible. She generally isn't interested in pictures or autographs, but she will talk to you. If you get a conversation going that she is somewhat interested in, she will usually open up to pictures and autographs. Rating: 5.

## Meg Ryan

Meg Ryan became a major star with the release of *When Harry Met Sally* in 1989. Before that she had been in a number of good films, including *Top Gun* with Tom Cruise, and the very funny *Armed and Dangerous* with John Candy. Since her big hit with *When Harry Met Sally* Meg has starred in a number of high-profile films, including the huge hit of 1993, *Sleepless in Seattle*, with Tom Hanks. She is married to actor Dennis Quaid. A good conversation starter with Meg would be her time on the soap opera *As the World Turns* or her short-lived stint on a television sitcom entitled *One of the Boys* in 1982. Meg was born in Fairfield, Connecticut, on November 19, 1961. She is very approachable and is terrific to meet. She is also happy to sign autographs or take pictures. Rating: 8.

## Arnold Schwarzenegger

Arnold Schwarzenegger is one of the biggest box office draws of all time. In 1982, after five tries, he finally had a hit on his hands with *Conan the Barbarian*. In 1984, he was propelled to the top of his field with the release of *The Terminator*. He has since starred in a number of huge box office successes, including *Total Recall*, *The Running Man*, and *True Lies*. A good conversation starter with Arnold would be his selection as chairman of the President's Council on Physical Fitness by George Bush. Another topic would be his wife, Maria Shriver. And still another topic would be the success of his restaurant chain, Planet Hollywood. Arnold was born in Austria on July 30, 1947. He is difficult to approach. He uses a slick method of refusing pictures and autographs without looking like a bad guy: When asked for a picture he says "Sure," but keeps on walking. Catch him in a good mood and use a good opening line, and you will be able to get a picture with him. Rating: 5.

Steve with Arnold Schwarzenegger

## *Steven Seagal*

Steven Seagal is one of the top action-movie actors. He has starred in the hits *Above the Law*, *Hard to Kill*, *On Deadly Ground*, and his biggest success, *Under Seige*. Seagal is a martial arts expert who taught the skill to many of Hollywood's elite. One of his students was superagent Mike Ovitz, who runs the top agency in Hollywood, Creative Artists. Ovitz decided he wanted to make a star of Seagal and put together a deal for Seagal to star in, cowrite, and coproduce his first attempt in films, *Above the Law*. Ovitz's deal proved successful—as do most of Ovitz's deals—and Seagal has continued to land hit after hit. A good conversation starter with Steven would be his high school in Buena Park, California, where he was a Howling Coyote. Seagal was born in Detroit on April 10, 1951. He was married to actress Kelly LeBrock (*Weird Science*). Seagal is fairly accessible and usually has no problem with autographs and pictures. Rating: 7.

## *Jerry Seinfeld*

Jerry Seinfeld has become one of the hottest stars on television thanks to his top-rated sitcom, *Seinfeld*. The show began in 1990, but was consistently beaten by *Home Improvement*. Once it was moved to follow *Cheers*, it raced up the ratings list to number two. Since then it has been one of the most popular shows on television. Jerry was a very successful stand-up comedian before his role on *Seinfeld*, and, in fact, the character he plays on the show is also a stand-up comedian. A good conversation starter with Jerry would be his short time as Frankie on the sitcom *Benson* during the 1980–1981 season. Jerry was born in New York on April 29, 1957. He is happy to sign autographs and take pictures and genuinely seems down-to-earth. Rating: 8.

## Paul Shaffer

Paul Shaffer is best known as David Letterman's band leader. Paul has been directing the music for *Late Night With David Letterman* and, more recently, for the *Late Show With David Letterman*, for over ten years. Paul is also a very successful musician and has appeared on many albums and tours with top artists, including Robert Plant's, Honeydrippers project. A good conversation starter with Paul would be anything about Canada, his native country. Paul was born on November 28, 1949. He is a very interesting celebrity and is full of stories and anecdotes about the music industry and musicians, since he has worked with almost everybody at one time or another. Paul is always ready to sign autographs or pose for pictures. Rating: 9.

## Garry Shandling

Garry Shandling became famous as the star of the *Garry Shandling Show*. His most recent hit, on HBO, is the weekly series the *Larry Sanders Show*, which stars Garry as a talk show host. A good conversation starter with Shandling would be about his early television appearance on *Sanford and Son*. Garry was born in Chicago on November 29, 1949. He is one of the most obnoxious celebrities Steve and I have ever met. Good luck approaching Garry, as he seems very stuck on himself. Rating: 1.

## Frank Sinatra

Frank Sinatra became famous for his incredible singing voice. He has had a number of hits, including "My Way," "Strangers in the

Night," and "Somethin' Stupid," but is best remembered as a classic crooner. He has also starred in dozens of feature films and, in fact, has won two Oscars, one for Best Actor for his role in *From Here to Eternity*. Legend has it that he had to beg for the role in *From Here to Eternity* and agreed to star in it for under $10,000. A good conversation starter for Frank would be his trouble with the Grammy Awards. He boycotted the awards for many years; then, in 1994, the Grammys gave him a Lifetime Achievement Award. He showed up at the ceremony and was rudely cut short during his acceptance speech. Frank was born in Hoboken, New Jersey, on December 12, 1915. He does not spend too much time with the public and is difficult to approach. Rating: 3.

## Christian Slater

Christian Slater is one of the hottest young actors working today. He had been in five films before gaining national attention in *Pump Up the Volume*. He has since starred in many hits, including *Young Guns II*, *Untamed Heart*, *True Romance*, *Interview With the Vampire*, and, most recently, *Murder in the First*. A good conversation starter with Christian would be his appearance on the daytime soap *One Life to Live* in 1976. Slater was born Christian Hawkins in New York City on August 18, 1969. He is fairly accessible and usually has no problems with autographs or pictures. Rating: 8.

## Aaron Spelling

Aaron Spelling is one of the most successful television producers of all time. His list of credits includes many of the biggest hits television has ever seen. Spelling is the man who brought us *The Mod Squad*, *Starsky and Hutch*, *S.W.A.T.*, *Charlie's Angels*, *The Love Boat*, *Fantasy Island*, *Dynasty*, *Beverly Hills 90210*, and *Melrose Place*. A good conversation starter with Aaron would be the famous parties at his fifty-thousand-square-foot home in Beverly Hills. He hosted a party for Prince Charles, and a Halloween party where everyone dressed up like a character from one of his shows. Aaron was born in Dallas on April 22, 1928. He is very approachable and has no problem taking pictures or signing autographs. Rating: 9.

## Steven Spielberg

Steven Spielberg has emerged as Hollywood's leading director. In 1993, he won Academy Awards for Best Picture and Best Director for his film *Schindler's List*. That same year he released *Jurassic Park*, which became the biggest money-maker of all time. Spielberg is no stranger to commercial success. Many of his films rank right at the top of the money-makers list, including: *Jaws*, *Close Encounters of the Third Kind*, *Raiders of the Lost Ark* and its sequels, *E.T.: The Extra-Terrestrial*, *The Color Purple*, and *Hook*. A good conversation starter with Spielberg would be his work in animation. He has produced full-length cartoon movies, including *An American Tail*, *The Land Before Time*, and *We're Back!* Another topic would be Dive, the restaurant he owns in Century City, California. Spielberg was born in Cincinnati on December 18, 1947. He has been winning every award possible for the last two years and is a regular at the awards shows. This makes him very accessible. He seems to have no problem signing autographs and taking pictures. Rating: 8.

## Sylvester Stallone

Sylvester Stallone had played uneventful roles in movies for over five years when he went to the studios to sell a screenplay he had written. A movie studio was interested and offered Stallone $100,000 for the rights to the story. Although living in a trailer and eating cans of tuna, Stallone turned down the offer. He had written his script, *Rocky*, for himself and wanted to star in the film. After negotiations with the movie company in which the studio raised its offer to $250,000, the studio finally relented and gave Stallone very little money, but the coveted starring role. The film was released in 1976 and became a blockbuster. Stallone won the Academy Award for Best Picture and was nominated for Best Actor and Best Screenplay. Since then, Stallone has starred in many blockbuster, high-budget films, including *Rambo* and its sequels, *Cliffhanger*, *Demolition Man*, and *The Specialist*. A good conversation starter with Stallone would be his restaurant chain, Planet Hollywood. Stallone was born in New York on July 6, 1946. He is very funny in person and is open to autographs and pictures. Rating: 8.

## John Stamos

John Stamos became famous as Uncle Jessie on the hit television show *Full House*. Since he started on the show in 1987, John has become a huge hit with the teenage crowd. He got his start as Blackie on the daytime soap opera *General Hospital*. A good conversation starter with John could be his starring role in *Dreams*, a sitcom that lasted all of three weeks. John is also an accomplished musician: When his schedule allows, he plays drums for the Beach Boys, and he was also in a band called BB4 in the early eighties. John was born in Cypress, California, on August 19, 1963. He is very approachable and is willing to talk with the public, sign autographs, and take pictures. Rating: 9.

## Howard Stern

Howard Stern has gained fame as the top-rated radio personality in New York for many years. In the early 1990s he expanded his program to Los Angeles and quickly hit number one there as well. He is now heard in over twenty cities and is a huge success in most. He has had a top-rated television program, the *Howard Stern Show*, which he pulled from the air despite the fact that its ratings were consistently better than its competition, *Saturday Night Live*. Howard released a bestselling book, *Private Parts*, in 1993, which was the fastest-selling book of all time for its publisher Simon & Schuster. He is now in development on a feature film based on the book. He is commonly referred to as the King of All Media. A good conversation starter with Stern would be his annual broadcasts from the Rainbow Room during the after-party for the Grammy Awards. Another topic would be his now-famous producer Gary Dell'Abate. Stern is surprisingly generous when it comes to autographs and pictures. Rating: 9.

## Rod Stewart

Rod Stewart has produced hit songs for other people since the early seventies and his own songs have been huge hits, too. Some of his most popular are: "Do You Think I'm Sexy?," "Maggie May," "Hot Legs," and "Some Guys Have All the Luck." A good conversation starter with Rod would be anything about soccer, as he is a huge fan.

Another topic would be his long-time manager Randy Phillips. Rod played to one of the largest crowd of all time—three million people in Brazil on New Year's Eve, December 31, 1994. He was born in England on January 10, 1945. He is married to supermodel Rachel Hunter. Rod is very accessible and usually has no problem with pictures and autographs. Rating: 8.

## Sting

Sting became famous as the lead singer of the rock band the Police. The Police had a short but very successful career which included the hit songs "Every Breath You Take," "Da Doo Doo Doo (Da Da Da Da)," "Message in a Bottle," and "Roxanne." After the Police broke up, Sting began a solo career that has also been very successful. Additionally, Sting has appeared in a handful of feature films, including *Dune*, *The Bride*, and *Quadrophenia*. Sting's real name is Gordon Sumner. He was born in England on October 2, 1951. Sting is nice enough in person and generally has no problem with pictures or autographs. Rating: 7.

## Sharon Stone

Sharon Stone had appeared in three movies before making a significant impact in the Arnold Schwarzenegger film *Total Recall*. Her next big film, 1992's *Basic Instinct*, solidified her as one of the biggest box office draws in Hollywood. Since then she has starred with Sylvester Stallone in *The Specialist*, and with Richard Gere in *Intersection*, among a handful of other films. A good conversation starter with Sharon would be her role in *Bay City Blues* in 1983. She played Cathy St. Marie on the television show, which was about a minor league baseball team and lasted less than a month. Sharon was born in Meadville, Pennsylvania, on March 10, 1958. She is very approachable and has absolutely no problem with pictures and autographs. Rating: 9.

## John Travolta

John Travolta first became famous as Vinnie Barbarino on the hit television show *Welcome Back Kotter*. In 1978, he became a major motion picture star with his performance in the movie *Grease*, with Olivia Newton-John. In 1977, he started a cultural phenomenon called disco with his movie *Saturday Night Fever*. He earned an Oscar nomination for his role. He started a huge fad again with the release of his 1980 film *Urban Cowboy*—after its success, bars were installing bull-riding machines, and everyone was wearing cowboy hats and boots. Travolta's career slowed down a bit until *Look Who's Talking* in 1990. After another slow period, he exploded back into the limelight with 1994's *Pulp Fiction*. A good conversation starter with Travolta would be his marriage to actress Kelly Preston, or his love of flying—he owns three private airplanes. Travolta was born in Englewood, New Jersey, on February 18, 1954. He is very gracious and is willing to take pictures and sign autographs. Rating: 8.

## Jean Claude Van Damme

Jean Claude Van Damme has become a big hit as an action-film star. He has starred in the hits *Universal Soldier*, *Nowhere to Run*, and *Hard Target*. Jean Claude's real name is Jean Claude Van Vorenberg. He changed his name to Frank Cujo, but then thought better of it after the release of Stephen King's film *Cujo*. A good conversation starter with Jean Claude would be his penchant for Budweiser beer. Another topic could be the unbelievable coincidence that his birthday falls on the same day as mine. Jean Claude was born in Belgium on October 18, 1960. He is happy to take pictures and sign autographs. Jean Claude seems rather quiet in person, but also seems grateful for the opportunity to talk if you initiate a conversation. Rating: 8.

## Eddie Van Halen

Eddie Van Halen is the celebrity guitar player for the highly successful rock band Van Halen. He is considered one of the greatest rock guitarists ever by the industry. A good topic of conversation with Eddie would be a very early bootleg of a Van Halen concert, taped at the Pasadena Civic Center in which the band was introduced as "Van Halaman." Additionally, you might mention the theme song he wrote for his wife Valerie Bertinelli's sitcom, *Sydney*. He was born January 26, 1957, in Holland. Eddie is rather unapproachable. We have seen him turn down many picture and autograph requests. He will be more agreeable if you can get a conversation going first. Rating: 3.

# Eddie Vedder

Eddie Vedder has recently become famous as the lead singer of the rock band Pearl Jam, which is currently one of the bestselling bands. His first album release with Pearl Jam, entitled *Ten*, produced a slew of hit songs on alternative radio. Their follow-up release, *Vs.*, debuted in the number one position on the sales charts. In 1994, Pearl Jam released their third CD, *Vitalogy*, which again was immediately number one. A good conversation starter with Vedder would be his personal fight against Ticketmaster, or his recent appearance at the 1994 Rock and Roll Hall of Fame, where he played with inductee Neil Young. Vedder's birth name is Eddie Mueller, but he uses his mother's maiden name, Vedder. He was born in Chicago. Eddie is not interested in being a celebrity and would prefer to make friends instead of fans. Approach him correctly and you can hang out all night. Rating: 5.

# Robin Williams

Robin Williams is best known now for his starring roles in feature films. He has had hits with *Mrs. Doubtfire*, *Hook*, *Good Morning, Vietnam*, and *Awakenings*. Williams began as a stand-up comedian and hit the big time with the television series *Mork and Mindy*, a spinoff of *Happy Days*. His first starring movie role was in 1980, in the movie *Popeye*, which bombed. A good conversation starter with Robin would be the fact that he was a regular on the television show *Laugh-In* in 1979. Williams was born in Chicago on July 21, 1952. He seems to be very full of himself and is not very congenial. His television appearances on charity functions such as *Comic Relief* show him to be very fun-loving and nice, but don't let that fool you. Steve and I have seen Robin in action in real life and he is anything but nice to the public. Unless you can immediately help his career or give him something he wants, you probably shouldn't bother. Rating: 2.

# Oprah Winfrey

Oprah Winfrey has redefined daytime talk shows. As the star of the *Oprah Winfrey Show* she is able to flex her considerable talent as host. She is creative, smart, and very entertaining. She is also a very talented actress, as was demonstrated by her incredible performance in *The Color Purple*, which earned her an Academy Award nomination. A good conversation starter with Oprah would be her appearance on the daytime soap opera *All My Children*. Another topic would be her recent jogging career—she has been running in marathons. Oprah was born on January 29, 1954, in Kosciusko, Mississippi. She is extremely open to meeting the public. She is always willing to take pictures and sign autographs. Rating: 9.

# 11

# Local Encounters

**E**very method outlined in this book can be used across the country and around the world. Celebrities can be found everywhere from spring break in Florida, to concerts, sporting events, and movie locations in every city.

Use the tips in this book to get passes to the Garth Brooks concert as it passes through town, or gain access to the set of Tom Cruise's new movie, which is filming on location nearby. If you look for celebrities, you will find them. What follows is a list of phone numbers we have compiled to help you get started. The list includes hotels and restaurants that celebrities frequent, limousine services, newspapers, record companies, and a variety of other useful information. Although we've done our best to get things correct this list may not be perfect and we can't guarantee the accuracy of its contents. If the number is no longer accurate, then just call information and get the new one.

## Baltimore

*Limousine Companies*

Carey Limo (410) 837–1234
Chesapeake (410) 366–3000
Harbor Limo (410) 477–8144
Steppin' Out (410) 592–3987

## Health Clubs

Downtown Athletic (410) 332–0906
Gold's Gym (410) 252–8271
Merritt Athletic (410) 821–0160
Powerhouse Gym (410) 636–7440

## Hotels

Baltimore Marriott Inner Harbor (410) 962–0202
The Columbia Inn (410) 730–3900
Hyatt Regency Baltimore (410) 528–1234
Society Hill Hopkins (410) 235–8600
Stouffer's Harborplace Hotel (410) 547–1200

## Restaurants

Chart House (410) 539–6616
Diamimmo's Italian Restaurant (410) 727–6876
Louie's (410) 962–1224
Shogun (410) 962–1130
Tio Pepe (410) 539–4675

## Concert and Event Locations

Baltimore Arena (410) 347–2020
Kraushaar Auditorium (410) 337–6333
Merriweather Post Pavilion (410) 730–2424
Michael's Eighth Avenue (410) 768–7901
Pier 6 Concert Pavilion (410) 625–3100
Shriver Hall (410) 516–8209
The Towson Center (410) 830–2315

## Press

*Baltimore Sun* (410) 332–6000
*City Paper* (410) 523–2300
*Maryland Musician* (410) 444–3776

## Television Stations

ABC (410) 466–0013
CBS (410) 467–3000
Fox (410) 467–4545
NBC (410) 377–2222

## Radio Stations

Alternative WHFS 99.1 FM (301) 306–0991
Classic Rock WGRX 100.7 FM (410) 435–9487
Country WPOC 93.1 FM (410) 366–3693

Hard Rock WXZL 103.1 FM (410) 269–7779
Rock WIYY 97.9 FM (410) 889–0098
Top Forty WERQ 92.3 FM (410) 523–6900

# Boston

*Limousine Companies*

Cap's Auto Livery (617) 523–0727
Carey Limo (617) 623–8700
Cloud Nine (508) 384–8094
Fifth Avenue (617) 286–0555

*Health Clubs*

Beacon Hill Athletic Club (617) 720–2422
Fitcorp (617) 542–1010
Gold's Gym (617) 536–6066
Sky Club (617) 426–1212

*Hotels*

Boston Harbor Hotel (617) 439–7000
The Charles Hotel (617) 864–1200
The Colonnade (617) 424–7000
Ritz-Carlton Boston (617) 536–5700
Swissotel Boston (617) 451–2600

*Restaurants*

Aujourd'Hui (617) 451–1392
Biba (617) 426–7878
Hard Rock Cafe (617) 424–7625
Michela's Restaurant (617) 225–2121
Top of the Hub (617) 536–1775

*Concert and Event Locations*

Boston Garden (617) 227–3200
Orpheum Theater (617) 482–0651
Wang Center (617) 482–9393

*Press*

*Boston Globe* (617) 929–2000
*Boston Herald* (617) 426–3000
*Boston* Magazine (617) 262–9700
*Boston Rock* (617) 244–6803
*Improper Bostonian* (617) 232–3507
*The Tab* (617) 964–2400

*Television Stations*

    ABC (617) 449–0400
    CBS (617) 725–0777
    Fox (617) 326–8825
    NBC (617) 787–7000

*Radio Stations*

    Alternative WFNX 101.7 FM (617) 595–6200
    Classic Rock WZLX 100.7 FM (617) 267–0123
    Country WCLB 105.7 FM (617) 375–2100
    Rock WCGY 93.7 FM (508) 683–7171
    Top Forty WJMN 94.5 FM (617) 290–0009

# Chicago

*Limousine Companies*

    Carey Limo (312) 663–1220
    Exotic Limo (312) 427–2141
    Gold Coast Limo (312) 588–8000
    Regency (312) 281–9400

*Health Clubs*

    Athletic Club Illinois Center (312) 616–9000
    Jamnastics (312) 477–8400
    Lehmann's Sports Club (312) 871–8300
    North Pier Athletic Club (312) 464–3300

*Hotels*

    The Drake (312) 787–2200
    Fairmont Hotel (312) 565–8000
    Hotel Nikko Chicago (312) 744–1900
    Hyatt Regency Suites (312) 337–1234
    Le Meridien (312) 266–2100

*Restaurants*

    Benkay (312) 836–5490
    Bub City Crabshack and Bar BQ (312) 266–1200
    Hard Rock Cafe (312) 943–2252
    Moosehead Bar and Grill (312) 649–9113
    Scoozi (312) 943–5900

*Concert and Event Locations*

    Aragon Entertainment Center (312) 561–9500
    Arie Crown Theatre (312) 791–6000

Metro (312) 549–0203
The Pavilion UICC (312) 413–5700
Regal Theater (312) 721–9301
The Riviera (312) 275–6800
Soldier Field (312) 294–2200

*Press*

*Chicago* Magazine (312) 222–8999
*Chicago Music* Magazine (312) 525–7553
*Chicago Sun Times* (312) 321–3000
*Chicago Tribune* (312) 222–3232

*Television Stations*

ABC (312) 750–7777
CBS (312) 944–6000
Fox (312) 565–5532
NBC (312) 836–5555

*Radio Stations*

Alternative WCBR 92.7 FM (708) 255–5800
Classic Rock WCKG 105.9 FM (312) 781–7300
Country WUSN 99.5 (312) FM 649–0099
Hard Rock WWBZ 103.5 FM (312) 861–8100
Rock WLUP 97.9 FM (312) 440–5270
Top Forty WBBM 96.3 FM (312) 944–6000

# Cincinnati

*Limousine Companies*

M & M Limo (513) 451–7936
Park Avenue Limo (513) 689–5466
Superior Limo (513) 761–7734
Top Shelf Limo (513) 221–0074

*Health Clubs*

Carew Tower Health (513) 651–1142
Mid-Town Athletic Club (513) 351–3000
Moore's Fitness World (513) 381–2323
Queen City Racquet (513) 771–2835

*Hotels*

Cincinnatian Hotel (513) 381–3000
Garfield House Suite Hotel (513) 421–3355
Hyatt Regency (513) 579–1234

Omni Netherland Plaza (513) 421–9100
Vernon Manor Hotel (513) 281–3300

### Restaurants

The Celestial (513) 241–4455
Champ's Italian Chop House (513) 579–1234
Crockett's and The River Cafe (606) 581–2800
Funky's Blackstone Grille (513) 321–0010
Izzy's (513) 721–4241

### Concert and Event Locations

Cincinnati Gardens (513) 631–7793
Music Hall (513) 721–8222
Riverbend Music Center (513) 232–5882
Riverfront Coliseum (513) 241–1818
Shoemaker Center (513) 556–2170
Taft Theatre (513) 721–0411
Timberwolf Amphitheater (513) 241–5600

### Press

*Cincinnati Enquirer* (513) 721–2700
*Cincinnati* Magazine (513) 421–4300
*Cincinnati Post* (513) 352–2000
*Downtowner* (513) 241–9906

### Television Stations

ABC (513) 763–5500
CBS (513) 721–9900
Fox (513) 772–1919
NBC (513) 352–5000

### Radio Stations

Alternative WOXY 97.7 FM (513) 863–5665
Classic Rock WOFX 94.9 FM (513) 241–9500
Country WUBE 105.1 FM (513) 721–1050
Rock WEBN 102.7 FM (513) 621–9326
Top Forty WKRQ 101.9 FM (513) 763–5500

# Dallas

### Limousine Companies

Carey of Dallas (214) 638–4828
Limos by Jan (214) 327–6616

Limos/Las Colinas (214) 570–5808
RSVP Limo (214) 494–6867

### Health Clubs

Austin Gym (214) 231–8414
Bally's Health Club (214) 871–7700
Centrum Sports Club (214) 522–4100

### Hotels

Fairmont Hotel (214) 720–2020
Four Seasons Resort and Club (214) 717–0700
Grand Kempinski (214) 386–6000
Hotel Cresent Court (214) 871–3200
Melrose Hotel (214) 521–5151

### Restaurants

Baby Routh (214) 871–2345
Dakota's (214) 740–4001
Lombardi's (214) 954–0803
Nate's Steak and Seafood (214) 701–9622
Sfuzzi (214) 871–2606

### Concert and Event Locations

The Basement (214) 987–9922
Bomb Factory (214) 748–2662
Cotton Bowl (214) 565–9931
Dallas Convention Center Arena (214) 939–2700
Fair Park Coliseum (214) 565–9931
Reunion Arena (214) 670–1395
Starplex Amphitheater (214) 421–1111

### Press

*Dallas Morning News* (214) 977–8222
*Dallas Observer* (214) 637–2072
*Jam* Magazine (817) 540–4847
*Texas Monthly* (214) 871–7717

### Television Stations

ABC (214) 748–9631
CBS (214) 720–4444
Fox (214) 634–8833
NBC (214) 745–5555

*Radio Stations*

Alternative KDGE 94.5 FM (214) 580–9400
Classic Rock KZPS 92.5 FM (214) 770–7777
Country KPLX 99.5 FM (214) 526–2400
Hard Rock KDZR 99.1 FM (214) 406–1991
Rock KEGL 97.1 FM (214) 869–9700
Top Forty KHKS 106.1 FM (214) 891–3400

# Detroit

*Limousine Companies*

Carey Statewide (313) 946–5466
Continental Limo (313) 626–8282
Gambino (313) 728–8736
Michigan Limo (313) 546–6112

*Health Clubs*

Fitnesse (313) 540–2535
Vic Tanny (313) 557–1400
Workout Company (313) 855–1033

*Hotels*

Atheneum Hotel (313) 962–2323
Ritz-Carlton Dearborn (313) 441–2000
River Place Inn (313) 259–2500
Townsend Hotel (313) 642–7900
Westin Hotel (313) 568–8000

*Restaurants*

Fishbones (313) 965–4600
Rattlesnake Club (313) 567–4400
333 East (313) 222–7404
Van Dyke Place (313) 821–2620
The Whitney (313) 832–5700

*Concert and Event Locations*

Palace of Auburn Hills (313) 337–8600
Phoenix Plaza Amphitheater (313) 335–4850
Pontiac Silverdome (313) 456–1600
The Ritz (313) 778–8150
Royal Oak Music Theater (313) 546–7610
Saint Andrews Hall (313) 961–6358
State Theatre (313) 961–5450

*Press*

> *Detroit Monthly* (313) 446–6000
> *Detroit News* (313) 222–2095
> *Metro Times* (313) 961–4060
> *Orbit* Magazine (313) 541–3900

*Television Stations*

> ABC (313) 827–7777
> CBS (313) 557–2000
> Fox (313) 350–5050
> NBC (313) 222–0444

*Radio Stations*

> Alternative CIMX 88.7 FM (519) 966–7000
> Classic Rock WCSX 94.7 FM (313) 398–7600
> Country WWWW 106.7 FM (313) 259–4323
> Rock WLLZ 98.7 FM (313) 855–5100
> Top Forty WKQI 95.5 FM (313) 967–3750

# Houston

*Limousine Companies*

> Allantra Limo (713) 660–0942
> Brigadier Limo (713) 686–1100
> Carey of Houston (713) 367–4759
> Sterling (713) 468–5466

*Health Clubs*

> Bodyrock (713) 522–0366
> Gold's Gym (713) 493–1874
> Hank's (713) 668–6219
> Memorial Athletic (713) 497–7570

*Hotels*

> Adam's Mark Hotel (713) 978–7400
> Four Seasons Houston Center (713) 650–1300
> La Colombe D'Or (713) 524–7999
> The Lancaster (713) 228–9500
> Stouffer Presidente Hotel (713) 629–1200

*Restaurants*

> Blue Water Grill (713) 526–7977
> 8.0 (713) 523–0880
> Hard Rock Cafe (713) 520–1134

Nino's (713) 522–5120
The Palm (713) 977–2544

*Concert and Event Locations*

The Astrodome (713) 799–9500
Backstage Club (713) 270–6602
Lone Star Amphitheater (713) 661–6139
Rockefeller's (713) 861–9365
Rockefeller's West (713) 977–5495
Sam Houston Coliseum (713) 247–1048
Southern Star Amphitheater (713) 799–1234

*Press*

*Concert Circuit* (713) 277–6626
*Houston Chronicle* (713) 220–7171
*Houston Post* (713) 840–5600
*Houston Press* (713) 624–1400

*Television Stations*

ABC (713) 666–0713
CBS (713) 526–1111
Fox (713) 626–2610
NBC (713) 771–4631

*Radio Stations*

Alternative KTRU 91.7 FM (713) 527–4050
Classic Rock KZFX 107.5 FM (713) 968–1000
Country KIKK 95.7 FM (713) 772–4433
Hard Rock KKZR 106.9 FM (713) 260–3600
Rock KLOL 101.1 FM (713) 526–6855
Top Forty KBXX 97.9 FM (713) 978–7328

# Kansas City, MO

*Limousine Companies*

American Limo (816) 471–6050
Overland Limo (913) 381–3504
Plaza Limo (816) 756–1700
Star Search Limo (816) 765–9032

*Health Clubs*

Athletic Club (913) 383–9060
Gold's Gym (816) 391–9888

Hyatt Health Club (816) 421–1234
Plaza Athletic Club (816) 756–0067

*Hotels*

Adam's Mark (816) 737–0200
Hyatt Regency Crown Center (816) 421–1234
Park Place Hotel (816) 483–9900
Ritz-Carlton Kansas City (816) 756–1500
Sheraton Suites (816) 931–4400

*Restaurants*

Fedora Cafe and Bar (816) 561–6565
Gojo Japanese Steak House (816) 561–2501
Plaza III (816) 753–0000
Red Dragon (816) 221–1388
Savoy Grill (816) 842–3890

*Concert and Event Locations*

Arrowhead Stadium (816) 924–9300
The Forum (816) 454–4545
Kemper Arena (816) 274–1900
Midland Center (816) 421–7501
Municipal Auditorium (816) 274–2900
Sandstone Amphitheater (913) 721–3400
Starlight Theater (816) 333–9481

*Press*

*Kansas City Globe* (816) 531–5253
*Kansas City New Times* (816) 753–7880
*Kansas City Star* (816) 234–4141

*Television Stations*

ABC (816) 221–9999
CBS (913) 677–5555
Fox (816) 753–4141
NBC (816) 753–4567

*Radio Stations*

Alternative KLZR 105.9 FM (913) 843–1320
Classic Rock KCFX 101.1 FM (913) 661–0101
Country KFKF 94.1 FM (913) 321–3200
Hard Rock KQRC 98.9 FM (913) 384–9900
Rock KYYS 102.1 FM (816) 561–9102
Top Forty KXXR 107.3 FM (816) 373–1073

# Las Vegas

*Limousine Companies*

Bell Trans (702) 739–7990
Las Vegas Limo (702) 739–8414
Presidential Limo (702) 731–5577

*Health Clubs*

Caesars Palace (702) 731–7110
Family Fitness West (702) 368–1111
Gold's Gym (702) 877–6966
Green Valley Athletic Club (702) 454–6000
World Gym (702) 435–5646

*Hotels*

Bally's Las Vegas Hotel (702) 739–4111
Caesars Palace (702) 731–7110
Golden Nugget Hotel and Casino (702) 385–7111
Las Vegas Hilton (702) 732–5111
The Mirage (702) 791–7111

*Restaurants*

Benihana (702) 732–5111
Bono's (702) 456–6248
Kokomo's (702) 791–7111
Rosewood Grille and Lobster House (702) 792–6719
Tony Roma's (702) 733–9914

*Concert and Event Locations*

Artemus W. Ham Concert Hall (702) 895–3801
Cashman Field Auditorium (702) 386–7100
Huntridge Performing Arts Center (702) 477–0242
Las Vegas Convention Center (702) 892–0711
Sam Boyd Silver Bowl (702) 895–3761
Thomas and Mack Center (702) 895–3761

*Press*

*Las Vegas Sun* (702) 385–3111
*Las Vegas Today* (702) 221–5000
*Review Journal* (702) 383–0211

*Television Stations*

ABC (702) 876–1313
CBS (702) 792–8888

Fox (702) 435–5555
NBC (702) 642–3333

*Radio Stations*

Alternative KUNV 91.5 FM (702) 895–3877
Classic Rock KKLZ 96.3 FM (702) 739–9600
Country KWNR 95.5 FM (702) 798–4004
Rock KOMP 92.3 FM (702) 876–1460
Top Forty KMZQ 100.5 FM (702) 731–5100

# Los Angeles

*Limousine Companies*

Carey International (800) 336–4646
Dav-El Los Angeles (310) 550–0070
Music Express (213) 849–2244
Starlite (310) 858–1060

*Health Clubs*

Gold's Gym (213) 462–7012
Martin Henry (310) 659–9200
Sports Connection (310) 450–4464
Voight Fitness (310) 854–0741

*Hotels*

Bel Age Hotel (310) 854–1111
Chateau Marmont Hotel (213) 656–1010
Mondrian Hotel (213) 650–8999
St. James Club and Hotel (213) 654–7100
Sunset Marquis Hotel and Villas (310) 657–1333

*Restaurants*

Atlas Bar and Grill (213) 380–8400
The Monkey Bar (213) 658–6005
Nicky Blair's (310) 659–0929
Spago (310) 652–4025
Sushi on Sunset (213) 656–3242

*Concert and Event Locations*

Anaheim Arena (714) 704–2400
Anaheim Stadium (714) 254–3100
Celebrity Theater (714) 535–2000
Coach House (714) 496–8930
Great Western Forum (310) 419–3100

Greek Theater (213) 665–5857
Hollywood Bowl (213) 850–2000
Hollywood Palladium (213) 962–7600
Irvine Meadows (714) 855–8096
Long Beach Convention Center (310) 436–3636
Los Angeles Memorial Coliseum (213) 748–6131
Los Angeles Sports Arena (213) 748–6131
Pacific Amphitheater (714) 546–4876
The Palace (213) 467–4571
Pasadena Civic Auditorium (818) 793–2122
Royce Hall (310) 825–2101
Universal Amphitheater (818) 777–3931
Wiltern Theater (213) 380–5005

### Press

*Bam* (213) 851–8600
*Daily Breeze* (310) 540–5511
*Hollywood Reporter* (213) 525–2000
*L.A. Weekly* (213) 667–2620
*Los Angeles Times* (213) 237–5000
*Orange County Register* (714) 835–1234
*Variety* (213) 857–6600

### Television Stations

ABC (310) 557–7777
CBS (213) 460–3000
Fox (213) 856–1000
NBC (818) 840–4444

### Radio Stations

Alternative KROQ 106.7 FM (818) 567–1067
Classic Rock KLSX 97.1 FM (213) 383–4222
Country KZLA 93.9 FM (818) 842–0500
Hard Rock KNAC 105.5 FM (310) 437–0366
Rock KLOS 95.5 FM (310) 840–4800
Top Forty KIIS 102.7 FM (213) 466–8381

# Memphis

### Limousine Companies

A Classic C'est La Vie Limo (901) 725–5466
Memphis Executive (901) 396–7733
Superior Limo (901) 327–2503
Tennessee Limo (901) 452–9026

## Health Clubs

French Riviera Spa (901) 276–2585
Healthplex (901) 227–7054
Peabody Athletic Club (901) 529–4161
The Q (901) 763–3265

## Hotels

Adam's Mark Hotel (901) 684–6664
East Memphis Hilton (901) 767–6666
Memphis Marriott Hotel (901) 362–6200
The Peabody (901) 529–4000
Sassafras Inn (800) 882–1897

## Restaurants

Automatic Slim's (901) 525–7948
B.B. King's Blues Club (901) 524–5464
Rendezvous (901) 523–2746
Dux (901) 529–4199
Owen Brennan's (901) 761–0990

## Concert and Event Locations

Ellis Auditorium (901) 576–1200
Mid-South Coliseum (901) 274–3982
Mud Island Amphitheater (901) 576–7206
Omni/New Daisy (901) 525–8979
Orpheum Theater (901) 525–3000
The Pyramid (901) 521–9675

## Press

*Commercial Appeal* (901) 529–2211
*Daily News* (901) 523–1561
*Memphis Flyer* (901) 521–9000
*Tri-State Defender* (901) 523–1818

## Television Stations

ABC (901) 320–1313
CBS (901) 577–0100
Fox (901) 278–2424
NBC (901) 726–0555

## Radio Stations

Alternative WQOX 88.5 FM (901) 385–4317
Country WGKX 105.9 FM (901) 767–6532
Rock WEGR 102.7 FM (901) 535–9103
Top Forty WMC 99.7 FM (901) 726–0555

# Miami

*Limousine Companies*

Ambassador (305) 931–3111
American VIP (305) 666–5466
Exec Q Car (305) 892–4444
Regal Limo/Carey (305) 945–5553

*Health Clubs*

Bally's (800) 695–8111
Downtown Athletic (305) 358–9988
Presidential Fitness (305) 967–9600
Scandinavian Health (305) 931–3181
Spa 66 (305) 525–6666

*Hotels*

The Alexander (305) 865–6500
Grand Bay Hotel (305) 858–9600
Occidental Park Suite Hotel (305) 374–5100
Seacoast Towes Hotel (305) 865–5152
Turnberry Isle Resort and Club (305) 932–6200

*Restaurants*

Chez Vendome (305) 443–4646
Dan Marino's American Sports Bar and Grill (305) 567–0013
Joe's Stone Crab (305) 673–0365
Shirt Tail Charlie's (305) 463–3474
Windows on the Green (305) 525–6666

*Concert and Event Locations*

Gusman Center (305) 374–8762
Knight International Center (305) 372–0277
Joe Robbie Stadium (305) 623–6100
Miami Amphitheater (305) 358–7550
Miami Arena (305) 530–4400
Orange Bowl (305) 643–7100

*Press*

*Miami Herald* (305) 350–2111
*Miami Review* (305) 377–3721
*Miami Times* (305) 757–1147
*Sun Sentinel* (305) 356–4000

*Television Stations*

ABC (305) 576–1010
CBS (305) 593–0606
Fox (305) 751–6692
NBC (305) 379–4444

*Radio Stations*

Classic Rock WZTA 94.9 FM (305) 624–9490
Country WQAM 560 FM (305) 621–4300
Rock WSHE 103.5 FM (305) 581–1580
Top Forty WVUM 90.5 FM (305) 284–5786

# Milwaukee

*Limousine Companies*

Aladdin Limo (414) 258–7686
Carey Limo (414) 332–9990
Elite (414) 476–1770
Royal Limo (414) 476–5870

*Health Clubs*

Nautilus Fitness Center (414) 462–4500
Downtown Club (414) 291–0444

*Hotels*

Marc Plaza Hotel (414) 271–7250
Milwaukee Marriott (414) 786–1100
Pfister Hotel (414) 273–8222
Sheraton Mayfair Inn (414) 257–3400
Wyndham Milwaukee Center (414) 276–8686

*Restaurants*

The Anchorage (414) 962–4710
Boulevard Inn (414) 765–1166
Giovanni's (414) 291–5600
Harold's (414) 481–8000
Knickerbocker on the Lake (414) 276–8500

*Concert and Event Locations*

Bradley Center (414) 227–0400
Marcus Amphitheater (414) 273–2680
Mecca Arena (414) 271–4000
Modjeska Theater (414) 383–1880

Performing Arts Center (414) 273–7121
The Rave (414) 342–7283
Riverside Theater (414) 271–2000
Shank Hall (414) 276–7288

*Press*

*Milwaukee* Magazine (414) 273–1101
*Milwaukee Sentinel* (414) 224–2000
*Milwaukee Star* (414) 449–4870
*Shepherd Express* (414) 276–2222

*Television Stations*

ABC (414) 342–8812
CBS (414) 355–6666
Fox (414) 442–7050
NBC (414) 332–9611

*Radio Stations*

Alternative WMSE 91.7 FM (414) 277–7247
Classic Rock WKLH 96.5 FM (414) 271–5511
Country WMIL 106.1 FM (414) 545–8900
Rock WLZR 102.9 FM (414) 453–4130
Top Forty WKTI 94.5 FM (414) 223–5339

# New York

*Limousine Companies*

Carey Limo (212) 599–1122
Dav-El (212) 645–4242
Mayfair Limo (212) 472–7500
Music Express (212) 736–5405

*Health Clubs*

Club La Raquette (212) 245–1144
David Barton (212) 727–0004
Physique (212) 315–2424
World Gym (212) 260–2534

*Hotels*

Essex House (212) 247–0300
The Peninsula (212) 247–2200
The Plaza (212) 759–3000
The Ritz-Carlton (212) 757–1900
The Waldorf–Astoria (212) 355–3000

*Restaurants*

Gotham Bar and Grill (212) 620–4020
Hard Rock Cafe (212) 459–9320
Planet Hollywood (212) 333–7827
Rainbow Room (212) 632–5100
Tavern on the Green (212) 873–3200

*Concert and Event Locations*

Apollo Theater (212) 864–0372
Carnegie Hall (212) 247–7800
Madison Square Garden (212) 465–6741
Paramount Theater (212) 465–6741
Radio City Music Hall (212) 247–4777
Roseland Ballroom (212) 247–0200

*Press*

*New York Post* (212) 815–8000
*New York Times* (212) 556–1234
*Newsday* (516) 843–2020
*Village Voice* (212) 475–3300

*Television Stations*

ABC (212) 456–7777
CBS (212) 975–4111
Fox (212) 452–5555
NBC (212) 664–4444

*Radio Stations*

Alternative WDRE 92.7 FM (516) 832–9400
Classic Rock WXRK 92.3 FM (212) 750–0550
Country WYNY 103.5 FM (212) 237–2900
Rock WBAB 102.3 FM (516) 587–1023
Top Forty WHTZ 100.3 FM (212) 239–2300

# Orlando

*Limousine Companies*

Coast to Coast (407) 282–5466
Mears Luxury (407) 422–5466
Town and Country (407) 828–3035
Transtar Limo (407) 856–7777

*Health Clubs*

Bally's Health (407) 678–1118
Bally's SW Orlando (407) 277–1144
Gold's Gym (407) 679–0800

*Hotels*

Grand Floridian Beach Resort (407) 824–3000
Hotel Royal Plaza (407) 828–2828
Park Plaza Hotel (407) 647–1072
Peabody Orlando (407) 352–4000
Swan Hotel (407) 934–3000

*Restaurants*

The Bubble Room (407) 628–3331
Christini's (407) 345–8770
Enzo's on the Lake (407) 834–9872
Kobe Japanese Steakhouse (407) 862–2888
Maison and Jardin (407) 862–4410

*Concert and Event Locations*

Performing Arts Center (407) 849–2577
Florida Citrus Bowl (407) 849–2560
Lakeland Civic Center Arena (813) 499–8111
Orange County Convention Center (407) 345–9898
Orlando Centroplex (407) 849–2020
Peabody Auditorium (904) 255–1314

*Press*

*Living in Orlando* (407) 539–3939
*Orlando* Magazine (407) 539–3939
*Orlando Sentinel* (407) 420–5000
*Weekly* (407) 645–5888

*Television Stations*

ABC (407) 841–9000
CBS (407) 291–6000
Fox (407) 644–3535
NBC (407) 645–2222

*Radio Stations*

Country WFIV 1080 FM (407) 847–4422
Rock WHTQ 96.5 FM (407) 295–3990
Top Forty WXXL 106.7 FM (407) 339–1067

# Philadelphia

*Limousine Companies*

Carey Limo (215) 492–8402
Dav-El (215) 259–2900
Frankford Limo (215) 743–2700
Limelight Limo (215) 342–5557

*Health Clubs*

Gold's Gym (215) 592–9644
Nautilus (215) 382–9010
Pennsport Club (215) 627–4900
The Sporting Club (215) 985–9876
Toppers Spa (215) 546–1850

*Hotels*

Four Seasons Hotel (215) 963–1500
The Latham (215) 563–7474
Ritz-Carlton (215) 563–1600
Warwick Hotel (215) 735–6000
Wyndham Franklin Plaza (215) 448–2000

*Restaurants*

Carolina's (215) 545–1000
Montserrat (215) 627–4224
Portofino (215) 923–8208
Sansom Street Oyster House (215) 567–7683
White Dog Cafe (215) 386–9224

*Concert and Event Locations*

Mann Music Center (215) 878–7707
Pennsylvania Convention Center (215) 574–2070
Philadelphia Civic Center (215) 823–5600
The Spectrum (215) 336–3600
Theater of the Living Arts (215) 922–1011
Veterans Stadium (215) 463–5191

*Press*

*City Paper* (215) 735–8444
*Philadelphia Inquirer* (215) 854–2000
*Philadelphia Tribune* (215) 893–4050
*Philadelphia Rock Guide* (215) 427–0583

*Television Stations*

ABC (215) 878–9700
CBS (215) 668–5700

       Fox (215) 925–2929

       NBC (215) 238–4700

*Radio Stations*

       Alternative WKDU 91.7 FM (215) 895–5917

       Classic Rock WYSP 94.1 FM (215) 668–9460

       Country WXTU 92.5 FM (215) 667–9000

       Rock WMMR 93.3 FM (215) 238–8000

       Top Forty WPLY 100.3 FM (215) 565–8900

# Phoenix

*Limousine Companies*

       Arizona Limo (602) 267–7097

       Hollywood Transportation (602) 242–9563

*Health Clubs*

       Beauvais Fitness (602) 829–6969

       City Square (602) 279–9633

       Western Reserve (602) 968–9231

       World Gym (602) 863–1125

*Hotels*

       Arizona Biltmore (602) 955–6600

       Hyatt Regency Scottsdale (602) 991–3388

       The Phoenician (602) 941–8200

       Scottsdale Princess Resort (602) 585–4848

       Wigwam Resort and Hotel (602) 935–3811

*Restaurants*

       Christo's (602) 264–1784

       Copper Creek Steak House and Grille (602) 253–7100

       The 8700 (602) 994–8700

       Orangerie (602) 954–2507

       Tony Roma's (602) 949–8900

*Concert and Event Locations*

       America West Arena (602) 379–2000

       Arizona Center (602) 271–4000

       ASU Activity Center (602) 965–3434

       Celebrity Theater (602) 267–0977

       Desert Sky Pavilion (602) 254–7200

       Phoenix Municipal Stadium (602) 262–7342

       Veterans Memorial Coliseum (602) 258–6711

*Press*

> *Arizona Republic* (602) 271–8000
> *Phoenix* Magazine (602) 248–8900
> *Scottsdale Progress* (602) 941–2300
> *Tempe Daily News* (602) 898–5680

*Television Stations*

> ABC (602) 266–5691
> CBS (602) 257–1234
> Fox (602) 243–4151
> NBC (602) 257–1212

*Radio Stations*

> Alternative KEDJ 106.3 FM (602) 266–1360
> Classic Rock KSLX 100.7 FM (602) 941–1007
> Country KNIX 102.5 FM (602) 966–6236
> Rock KUPD 97.9 FM (602) 838–0400
> Top Forty KOY 95.5 FM (602) 258–8181

# Pittsburgh

*Limousine Companies*

> Allegheny Limos (412) 731–8671
> Exter Limo (412) 653–5466
> First Class (412) 462–8000
> Rosewell Limo (412) 486–4491

*Health Clubs*

> City Club (412) 391–3300
> Exercise Warehouse (412) 621–1650
> South Hills Nautilus (412) 341–4363

*Hotels*

> Embassy Suites (412) 269–9070
> Hyatt Pittsburgh (412) 471–1234
> Pittsburgh Greentree Marriott (412) 922–8400
> Sheraton Inn Pittsburgh North (412) 776–6900
> Westin William Penn (412) 281–7100

*Restaurants*

> Common Plea (412) 281–5140
> Nico's Recovery Room (412) 681–9562
> Primanti Brothers (412) 263–2142
> Red Bull Inn (412) 787–2855
> Tin Angel (412) 381–1919

*Concert and Event Locations*

Palumbo Center (412) 396–6058
Benedum Center (412) 456–6666
Civic Arena (412) 642–1800
Heinz Hall (412) 392–4900
I. C. Light Amphitheater (412) 562–9900
Star Lake Amphitheater (412) 947–7827

*Press*

*Pittsburgh Courier* (412) 481–8302
*Pittsburgh* Magazine (412) 622–1360
*Pittsburgh Times* (412) 391–7222
*Post-Gazette* (412) 263–1100

*Television Stations*

ABC (412) 242–4300
CBS (412) 392–2200
Fox (412) 931–5300
NBC (412) 237–1100

*Radio Stations*

Alternative WPTS 98.5 FM (412) 648–7990
Classic Rock WRRK 96.9 FM (412) 922–9290
Country WMXP 100.7 FM (412) 381–8100
Rock WDVE 102.5 FM (412) 937–1441
Top Forty WBZZ 93.7 FM (412) 381–8100

# Seattle

*Limousine Companies*

Chester Dorsey (206) 322–7320
Park Place (206) 282–6997
Washington (206) 523–8000

*Health Clubs*

Fitness Limited (206) 728–1500
Nautilus Northwest (206) 443–9944
Pacific West Health (206) 643–0060
Seattle Club (206) 443–1111

*Hotels*

Alexis Hotel (206) 624–4844
Crowne Plaza Hotel (206) 464–1980
Edgewater Inn (206) 728–7000

Four Seasons Olympic (206) 621–1700
Salish Lodge (206) 888–2556

*Restaurants*

Adriatica (206) 285–5000
Cafe Flora (206) 325–9100
Metropolitan Grill (206) 624–3287
Labuznik (206) 441–8899
The Palm Court (206) 728–1000

*Concert and Event Locations*

Backstage (206) 781–2805
Crocodile Cafe (206) 448–2114
Kingdome (206) 340–2100
Paramount Theater (206) 682–1414
Seattle Center Arena (206) 684–7202
Under the Rail (206) 448–1900

*Press*

*Pandemonium* (206) 272–3319
*Post-Intelligencer* (206) 464–2121
*Seattle Times* (206) 464–2121
*Tacoma News Tribune* (206) 597–8742

*Television Stations*

ABC (206) 443–4000
CBS (206) 728–7777
Fox (206) 625–1313
NBC (206) 448–5555

*Radio Stations*

Alternative KNDD 107.7 FM (206) 622–3251
Classic Rock KZOK 102.5 FM (206) 281–5600
Country KRPM 106.1 FM (206) 649–0106
Rock KISW 99.9 FM (206) 285–7625
Top Forty KPLZ 101.5 FM (206) 223–5700

# St. Louis

*Limousine Companies*

Admiral Limo (314) 731–1707
Carey Limo (314) 946–4114
Jed Limo (314) 991–0767
Show Me Limo (314) 522–0888

*Health Clubs*

Gold's Gym (314) 968–3113
Mac's Body Shapers (314) 965–3392
Vic Tanny (314) 391–1600

*Hotels*

Doubletree Mayfair Suites (314) 421–2500
Hotel Majestic (314) 436–2355
Hyatt Regency St. Louis (314) 231–1234
Ritz-Carlton (314) 863–6300
Seven Gables Inn (314) 863–8400

*Restaurants*

Al's (314) 421–6399
Alligator Alley (314) 231–4287
Cicero's and the Basement Bar (314) 862–0009
Sansui (314) 367–2020
Webster Grill and Cafe (314) 962–0564

*Concert and Event Locations*

American Theater (314) 231–7000
The Arena (314) 644–0900
Fox Theater (314) 534–1678
Riverport Amphitheater (314) 298–9944
Sheldon Concert Hall (314) 533–9900
Stages (618) 874–4900

*Press*

*Riverfront Times* (314) 231–6666
*St. Louis Argus* (314) 531–1323
*St. Louis* Magazine (314) 231–7200
*St. Louis Post Dispatch* (314) 340–8000

*Television Stations*

ABC (314) 647–2222
CBS (314) 621–4444
Fox (314) 436–3030
NBC (314) 421–5055

*Radio Stations*

Alternative KPNT 105.7 FM (314) 231–1057
Classic Rock KSD 93.7 FM (314) 997–5594
Country WIL 92.3 FM (314) 436–1600
Rock KSHE 94.7 FM (314) 621–0095
Top Forty WKBQ 106.5 FM (314) 644–1380

# Washington, D.C.

*Limousine Companies*

Advantage Limo (301) 258–7755
Limoscene (301) 248–5466
Limousines Unlimited (301) 621–9191
Washingtonian (202) 338–5386

*Health Clubs*

Capital Fitness (301) 985–3111
City Fitness (202) 638–3539
Muscle Beach (202) 328–5201
Skyline Club (703) 820–4100
Sporting Club (703) 442–9150

*Hotels*

The Canterbury (202) 393–3000
Four Seasons Hotel (202) 342–0444
Guest Quarters Hotel (202) 333–8060
Latham Hotel (202) 726–5000
Ritz-Carlton (703) 415–5000

*Restaurants*

Cheesecake Factory (202) 364–0500
I Ricchi (202) 835–0459
Mr. K's (202) 331–8868
The Palm (202) 293–9091
Utopia (202) 483–7669

*Concert and Event Locations*

Arena Stage (202) 488–3300
Ford's Theater (202) 347–4833
John F. Kennedy Center for the Performing Arts (202) 416–8000
Merriweather Post Pavilion (410) 982–1800
RFK Stadium (202) 547–9077
US Air Arena (301) 350–3400

*Press*

*City Paper* (202) 332–2100
*Washington Post* (202) 334–6000
*Washington Times* (202) 636–3000
*Washingtonian* (202) 296–3600

*Television Stations*

ABC (202) 364–7777
CBS (202) 895–5999

Fox (202) 244–5151
NBC (202) 885–4000

*Radio Stations*

Alternative WHFS 99.1 FM (410) 880–4338
Classic Rock WJFK 106.7 FM (703) 691–1900
Country WMZQ 98.7 FM (202) 362–8330
Rock WWDC 101.1 FM (301) 587–7100
Top Forty WPGC 95.5 FM (301) 441–3500

# Important Numbers

*Record Labels, Television Studios, Production Companies, Movie Studios, Talent Agencies*

A&M Records – Los Angeles (213) 469–2411
A&M Records – New York (212) 333–1328
ABC Entertainment (212) 456–5669
American Comedy Network (203) 384–9443
Arista Records – Los Angeles (213) 655–9222
Arista Records – New York (212) 489–7400
Artists & Audience (212) 721–2400
ASCAP (800) 445–6138
Atlantic Records – Los Angeles (310) 205–7500
Atlantic Records – New York (212) 275–2000
Audience Development Group (616) 547–6704
Avalon Attractions (818) 708–8855
*BAM* Magazine (510) 934–3700
*Billboard* Magazine – Los Angeles (213) 525–2300
*Billboard* Magazine – New York (212) 764–7300
BMG (212) 930–4000
BMI (310) 659–9109
Buena Vista Pictures (818) 560–5000
Capitol Records – Los Angeles (213) 462–6252
Capitol Records – New York (212) 603–8700
Carolco Pictures (310) 289–7100
*Cash Box* Magazine (213) 464–8241
CBS Radio Network (212) 975–6714
*Circus* Magazine (212) 685–5050
Dick Clark Productions (818) 841–3003
Columbia Pictures (310) 280–8000
Columbia Records – Los Angeles (310) 449–2100
Columbia Records – New York (212) 833–8000

Creative Artists Agency (310) 288–4545
Def Jam Recordings (212) 229–5200
Delsener/Slater Enterprises (212) 249–7773
*Details* Magazine (212) 598–3710
DiLeo Entertainment (212) 956–2561
Disney Studios (818) 560–1000
Disney Records (818) 567–5325
Elektra Entertainment – Los Angeles (310) 288–3800
Elektra Entertainment – New York (212) 275–4000
Epic Records – Los Angeles (310) 449–2100
Epic Records – New York (212) 833–8000
ESPN Radio Network (212) 456–5688
*Esquire* Magazine (212) 459–7500
Geffen Records – Los Angeles (310) 278–9010
Geffen Records – New York (212) 841–8600
Giant Records (310) 289–5500
Global Satellite Network (818) 906–1888
The *Globe* (310) 207–7800
Goldenvoice (213) 656–4111
Bill Graham Presents (415) 541–0800
*Hits* Magazine (818) 501–7900
Hollywood Records (818) 560–5670
*Hollywood Reporter* (213) 525–2000
International Creative Management – Los Angeles (310) 550–4000
International Creative Management – New York (212) 556–5600
IRS Records (818) 508–3130
Liberty Records (615) 269–2000
*Life* Magazine (212) 522–1212
Linder/Balson Productions, Inc. (310) 471–1424
MCA Records – Los Angeles (818) 777–4000
MCA Records – New York (212) 841–8000
Mercury Records – Los Angeles (310) 996–7200
Mercury Records – New York (212) 333–8000
MGM/UA (310) 280–6000
Motown Records – Los Angeles (213) 468–3500
Motown Records – New York (212) 424–2000
MTV Networks (212) 258–8000
MTV News (212) 258–8826
*Music Connection* (213) 462–5772
NARAS (818) 843–8253
Nederlander Organization (213) 468–1710
New Audiences Productions (212) 595–5272

New Line Cinema (818) 995–6049
Nickelodeon (212) 258–8000
Orion Pictures (310) 282–0550
Paisley Park (612) 474–8555
Paramount Pictures (213) 956–5000
Parc Presentations (213) 468–1710
*People* Magazine (212) 522–1212
PolyGram – Los Angeles (310) 996–7200
PolyGram – New York (212) 333–8000
*Radio & Records* (310) 553–4330
RCA Records – Los Angeles (213) 468–4000
RCA Records – New York (212) 930–4000
Reprise Records (818) 846–9090
Rhino Records (310) 474–4778
*Rolling Stone* Magazine (212) 484–1616
Bill Silva Presents (619) 233–8400
Slash Records (213) 937–4660
*Spin* Magazine (212) 633–8200
*Sports Illustrated* (212) 522–1212
Stiefel-Phillips (310) 275–3377
TicketMaster (213) 480–3232
*Time* Magazine (212) 522–1212
T. J. Martell Foundation (212) 245–1818
Tommy Boy (212) 388–8300
Tower Records – Hollywood (310) 657–7300
Tower Records – New York (212) 799–2500
Tri-Star Pictures (310) 280–7700
Twentieth Century–Fox (310) 277–2211
Universal Studios (818) 777–1000
*US* Magazine (212) 484–1616
*USA Today* (703) 276–3400
*Variety* (213) 857–6600
VH-1 (212) 258–7800
Virgin Records – Los Angeles (310) 278–1181
Virgin Records – New York (212) 586–7700
Warner Brothers Pictures (818) 954–6000
Warner Brothers Records – Los Angeles (818) 846–9090
Warner Brothers Records – New York (212) 275–4500
Warner– Electra–Asylum (212) 275–4700
Westwood One (310) 204–5000
William Morris Agency – Los Angeles (310) 274–7451
William Morris Agency – New York (212) 586–5100